Ben Norman

Get to No.1 on Google

in easy steps

third edition

In easy steps is an imprint of In Easy Steps Limited
4 Chapel Court · 42 Holly Walk · Leamington Spa
Warwickshire · United Kingdom · CV32 4YS
www.ineasysteps.com

3rd Edition

Notice of Liability
Every effort has been made to ensure that this book contains accurate
and current information. However, In Easy Steps Limited and the
author shall not be liable for any loss or damage suffered by readers
as a result of any information contained herein.

Trademarks
All trademarks are acknowledged as belonging to their respective
companies.

Thanks
Thank you to my family, friends and colleagues for their continual
support which has enabled me to get to this position.
Also a special thank you to my girlfriend Samantha Noble for writing
support.

In Easy Steps Limited supports The Forest Stewardship Council (FSC),
the leading international forest certification organisation. All our titles
that are printed on Greenpeace approved FSC certified paper carry the
FSC logo.

Mixed Sources
Product group from well-managed
forests and other controlled sources
www.fsc.org Cert no. SGS-COC-005998
© 1996 Forest Stewardship Council

Printed and bound in the United Kingdom

ISBN 978-1-84078-533-3

Contents

1 Introduction to Google

Before you start optimizing your website, you need to know who you are optimizing for. This simple introduction will get you fully acquainted with Google, the world's most popular search engine.

Welcome to Google

Google is the world's most popular search engine, receiving more daily enquiries than any other. It has become the clear leader for search on the internet, performing nearly twice as many searches as its nearest rivals.

Google first appeared in 1997 as a very simple search box. Over the years it has retained its simplicity and has concentrated purely on making search more relevant. This is the reason for Google's massive growth and continued success.

Hot tip

To get the most relevant results when searching make sure your searches are as specific as possible.

Google has become an internet icon and in everyday conversations you will often hear people say "Just Google it". This shows the unprecedented impact that this simple search box has had on ordinary people's lives.

Google's core business is search, which it takes very seriously. This business consists of two main elements: natural search and sponsored listings.

Google, like any other business, will continue to grow and mature – an exciting future is open to the world's most popular search engine.

Google is an advertising vertical in its own right. If you use it properly, you'll be rewarded with a rich stream of highly converting traffic.

Businesses have come to learn very quickly that if their websites appear in the top search results of Google, the relevant traffic they attract will be colossal.

Any company can have their website appear in Google as long as it is deemed relevant. The problem most companies have is getting their websites into a position where they can be found.

How Google Works

Google uses an algorithm (See Glossary) to evaluate websites to determine their relevance.

Google's algorithm has hidden criteria, like its secret blend of spices that allow it to determine the most relevant website. The algorithm will weigh up various sites to see how relevant they are, and will score each one to see how closely it matches Google's ideal website before ranking it accordingly.

These points will be scored for details ranging from the title of the web page to the number of inward links it has pointing to it. The overall score is then assessed to see how relevant the page is for the searcher's specific search phrase. This will determine where a website will appear in the search engine's results.

To collect the information contained on websites, Google uses programs called spiders. Google's spiders will crawl the internet, moving from website to website via hyperlinks, and collecting data on their travels. Google will then take the information collected on each website and decide whether it is relevant enough to be placed in its search results and, if so, where.

Google will not automatically enter every website into its search results because this would make them less relevant, and relevance is Google's main objective.

Google's real power can be found in the algorithm which lies beneath its simple search box.

Beware

Google's complex algorithm means that it can and will detect attempts to fool it, and will penalize you.

Getting to Google's Heart

To get to Google's heart and have your site appear in this search engine is not the impossible feat people believe it to be.

There is one sure way to Google's heart and the top of this search engine, and that is through relevance.

Google has founded its success upon relevance, and if you follow their simple guidelines, achieving top positions is not beyond anyone's reach.

If you have a well-designed website that contains unique and relevant content, then the chances are Google will like your site.

The main reason people experience problems is that they do not effectively promote their websites to Google. Website owners often misrepresent their sites with non-descriptive titles and headings, and fail to utilize the free tools available.

This costly mistake can mean the difference between a top ten placement and coming in at 129th. The first will see your traffic and profits soar and the second will ensure that your site is virtually invisible.

There is another deciding factor that Google uses to determine rank positions and this involves link building from other sites. Google will find out how many links are pointing to your website from other websites and use this information to determine relevance.

If Google finds links to your website from other relevant websites and those links use relevant keywords, Google will recognize this.

This is why linking from relevant sites is very beneficial and will increase your chances of being found in Google's search results. This has proved crucial in the growth of Google and the continued relevance of its search results.

This is why, first and foremost, when creating and maintaining your website you must ensure that it remains relevant to your topic. If you stick to this simple yet effective rule, Google will find it easier to determine the relevance of your website.

Content is what Google wants and the more relevant to your subject the better. Give Google that and top rankings are sure to follow.

Hot tip

Keeping your keywords relevant will maximize your chances of gaining top ranking positions in Google's results.

Don't forget

Effective link building will increase your chances of a high position in Google.

Why is Google so Important?

If you could be at the top of only one search engine, the one to choose would be Google. The reason for this is very simple: more people use Google than any other search engine. Google receives millions of enquiries every day – missing out on the targeted traffic that passes through this search engine would be a grave mistake.

In a study of US search trends, Nielsen found that Google accounted for 64.2% of the searches conducted. This is more than half the market, as you can see from the graph shown below:

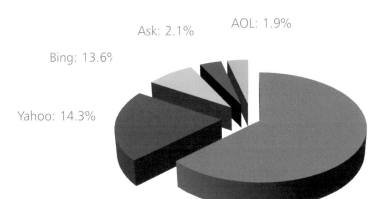

Ask: 2.1%

AOL: 1.9%

Bing: 13.6%

Yahoo: 14.3%

Google: 64.2%

Source: Nielsen

It is very difficult to bias or cheat your way into Google's clever algorithm.

People therefore find it reassuring to know that Google's results will be highly relevant to their searches. It helps people to build trust in the Google search engine and the websites it displays.

This gives Google the ability to advise people on the best websites to match their specific search queries. You can be assured of a large amount of targeted traffic if your website appears among the top results for your niche.

The best thing about this search traffic is that people landing at your website will be actively looking for your product or service, which means that you can be sure of a high conversion rate.

Why Not Just Pay Per Click?

Don't forget

Pay per click can seem an easy and fast way to achieve results but it is not always the most cost-effective option.

Hot tip

Naturally-ranked websites are more highly regarded than sponsored listings. Therefore, optimizing your site using relevant keywords and a user-friendly structure will be far more beneficial and will create more targeted traffic than pay per click would.

Beware

Approximately 65% of people never click on paid results so you must ensure your website is listed prominently in Google's natural listings.

Businesses, now more than ever, are using Google to market their products and services as they realize the abundance of targeted traffic it provides.

This then poses the question: do you optimize your website to appear in Google's natural search listings or do you pay to be placed in the sponsored listings?

It can sometimes seem an easy option just to pay for results, but is it really the right decision?

In a recent study, Google found that searchers were 72% more likely to click on a natural listing rather than a pay-per-click ad. This shows that although you can pay to get your website seen at the top of Google, it is not as effective as having it appear there naturally.

Searchers look for relevance in the ads they click on, in the same way that Google looks for relevance in the websites it shows in its natural listings. This is why natural search offers a much greater conversion rate: people know that the natural listings will tend to be more relevant to their search as they cannot be bought, only earned.

You can distinguish between Google's natural and sponsored listings as Google separates them in the following format:

The main benefit of natural listings is that they are free to earn and maintain. There are no click prices or fees as with pay per click. This is not to say that pay per click is not worth doing, just that natural listings are deemed more relevant and cost-effective.

What is Organic SEO?

Organic Search Engine Optimization, or Organic SEO as it is commonly called, is the process of optimizing your website to appear higher in the search engine's natural listings.

A dictionary definition of the word "optimization" is:

> "An act, process, or methodology of making something (as a design, system, or decision) as fully perfect, functional, or effective as possible; specifically: the mathematical procedures (as finding the maximum of a function) involved in this."
> *Source: Merriam Webster Online*

This is exactly what you need to do to your website to give it the prominence in the search engine that it deserves.

Search engine optimization involves the optimization of many different elements and, to optimize your website effectively, we will need to look at and optimize each of the following:

- Keywords
- Meta data
- Content
- Inward links
- Header tags
- Alt tags
- Internal links
- Website structure
- Website theme
- Website code

Once optimized, websites will stand a much greater chance of being found for their desired keywords. This is, after all, the whole reason for having a website.

There is no charge for appearing in Google's natural search engine listings, unlike other forms of advertising such as pay per click. This makes organic search engine optimization a very cost-effective method of advertising.

Don't forget

84% of searchers will never make it past page two of Google so you must ensure your website is listed within the first two pages of results.

13

Hot tip

It costs nothing to appear in Google's natural search results so ensure you make the most of this free advertising method.

The World as Google Sees it

Google sees the internet differently from the way searchers see it and it is important to understand this when designing your website, both initially and when optimizing it.

Paying attention to the coding of your website can often help when trying to find problems that are holding you back in Google.

Websites can often look fine at first glance but when you look at the world as Google sees it, by viewing the source code, you can see where the problems lie.

Website as we see it:

Website as Google sees it:

When your website is designed, make sure it is done in such a way that the page will validate (see p60-61), so that it looks good to searchers and so that Google can crawl it more easily.

Google takes information from your website code, not from the images we see, to assess your website. This is why it is important to ensure that your website code validates so that Google can find the information it needs.

Hot tip

When optimizing your website, view it as Google sees it – look at the source code – as this can make it easier to identify any errors in the coding.

Hot tip

To view the source code select View from the toolbar and then select Source.

14

Personalized Search

Over the last few years Google has been changing the search results and showing different people different results.

At first Google were only doing this to users that were signed into their Google accounts, but recently even non-signed-in users have been seeing personalized results.

Google is Personalizing results based on a number of factors including:

- Google+ activity

- Localization

- History

The effect of this is that essentially every users search could be unique and therefore different results could be seen for each user.

This is not to say that every search will be different, and in most cases the difference is very minimal.

An example could be that you do a new search for "widgets" and the top three results are widgets 1, widgets 2, and widgets 3. But if you were to do this search a few times, and click on widgets 3 the majority of the time, Google would begin to move that result higher up the list.

This is because when you search for the term "widgets" it knows you are more likely to be looking for that specific result based on your history and search behavior.

To combat personalized search website owners need to:

- Develop brand loyalty

- Make pages more accessible

- Ensure they are using the right keywords

- Create good, engaging website copy

- Increase website traffic

This can cause issues when you are checking your rankings, as the positions you see may differ slightly from what others see, but it is still an important metric.

Beware

Personalized search can result in you seeing different results when you check your website's rankings.

Ethical Optimization

There are two ways of optimizing your website to appear higher in the search engine's natural listings: the ethical way and the unethical way.

These are also known as "white hat SEO" and "black hat SEO". We will only cover the ethical way, using white hat SEO, as this is the only sustainable, long-term optimization technique.

To optimize using unethical methods can seem an attractive proposition as the results can be gained quickly, but these are often short-lived. The minute that Google realizes what you are doing, your website will be removed and your domain blacklisted.

This can cause immeasurable damage to your business as studies have shown that Google can blacklist the domain indefinitely. This could mean you would have to start with a new domain name and a new website.

It is important that when you are optimizing your website for Google you adhere to some simple, ethical rules to ensure that what you're doing is not against Google's code of practice. This will avoid future problems and ensure that everything that you do will be helping your ranking and not harming your site.

It is important to familiarize yourself with Google's webmaster guidelines as they will help you ensure you are not breaking any rules. These rules can be found on Google's home page by navigating to the About Google section. Once you have familiarized yourself with Google's guidelines, you will be in a much better position to decide on the ethical approach you wish to take to market your site, keeping Google's rules in mind.

It is very important that when optimizing websites you only use ethical search engine optimization and stay away from so called "black hat SEO" techniques. Using black hat techniques will ultimately prove beneficial to no one. Potential clients will be drawn to your site under false pretences, believing your site to contain content relevant to their specific search, but when arriving at your site will find this information non-existent.

This is the reason Google will penalize you for using such activities: the site would be irrelevant and so would jeopardize the quality of the search results.

2 Free Essential Tools and Services

To help Google find and place your website we are going to use a number of free tools. This will speed up the process and help you stay on the right track. We will introduce you to these tools in this chapter.

The Google Toolbar

The Google toolbar is a free search bar like many others available on the web but this one has some features that are worth their weight in gold.

The Google toolbar is positioned at the top of your browser and will give you valuable information about the website you are viewing.

Google's toolbar also acts as a search tool that is always available to you so, regardless of where you are on the web, you can start a new search without having to navigate to the Google homepage.

The Google toolbar is jam-packed full of useful features including:

- AutoFill
- AutoLink
- Translate
- Pop-up blocker
- Spell checker
- PageRank display
- Highlight search terms
- Word find buttons
- Bookmarks
- Send to
- Google account sign-in
- Gmail access
- Automatic update facility
- Optional privacy and security features

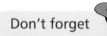

Don't forget

When you want to perform a search just use your Google toolbar – it will save you having to navigate to a search engine.

Hot tip

Do not worry about buying a pop-up blocker; with the Google toolbar you get it for free.

18

Download the Google Toolbar

1 Search for Google Toolbar from the Google homepage

Don't forget

To use the PageRank facility you must enable the feature in your privacy settings.

2 Select the Google Toolbar link

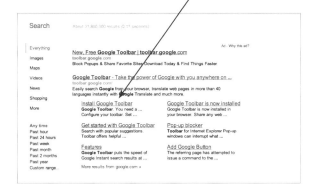

3 Download the Google Toolbar

4 Follow the install instructions and ensure that you enable the PageRank option

Backward Link Checker

The main and most valuable feature of the Google toolbar is its backward link checker. A backward link is simply a link that comes into your website from another website.

 Navigate to your website and right-click on the main page. Then select Page Info>Backward Links

Hot tip

See how your competition achieved their position by checking their backward links.

Using your backward link checker you will be able to:

- See who links to your website

- Assess the quality of the links

- Find out who your competition is

- See who links to your competition and how

- Source new links for your website

The Google toolbar makes finding out the answers to these questions easy by giving you a browser-based interface that is present every time you go online.

This means that you can simply navigate to your own website, or a competitor's website, and hit the backward link button to find out who is linking to the site.

Once you have found a page that links to the site, you can navigate to that page and find out even more information including:

- The PageRank of the website the link is on

- The anchor text used for the link

- Whether you can get a link from the page

This is a great benefit. Without this tool the process of assessing and finding incoming links would be much more difficult and time consuming.

Cached Pages Checker

Another very helpful tool when working out how you are faring in the optimization of your website is the Google cached page feature.

Hot tip

You can also check your cached pages using the button on the toolbar.

With this simple tool you can, at the touch of a button, find out exactly how Google sees your web page and when it was last crawled and cached.

The cached page checker shows you how Google sees a web page as it was when it last visited the website. It is important to note that the displayed image of a page may be different from the image we see. This may happen if cascading style sheets (CSS) were used to arrange items on the page. Google will only be interested in the content, and that is what it displays.

You can use this tool to check whether Google has noticed the changes you have made to the website and whether it has updated its cache.

Beware

Before making further changes to your website ensure that Google has your most recent website in its cache.

If you have made changes to your website and the cached page tool is showing your old page, it would indicate that Google has not yet updated and you should wait before you make any further alterations.

If Google has updated its cache but you are still not seeing effective results, this would indicate that Google doesn't think the changes make any difference to the site's relevance.

This tool will make sure that you do not overwrite your changes erroneously and will take the guesswork out of changing your website.

Google Account

If you want to use many of the Google tools and features then you will need to have a Google account.

Login Screen

Don't forget

You will need a Google account to take advantage of the free tools and services.

A Google account will offer you the ability to use and sign up for the following relevant services:

- Google Product Search

- AdWords

- AdSense

- Sitemaps

- Google Alerts

- Google Groups

- Analytics

- Personalized Search

Once your Google account has been activated, you will be able to access and utilize any of the tools you have signed up for. This is convenient as you will have one login that can be used for all of the tools.

This enables you to access all of your Google tools and services from one easy-to-manage account.

Google Webmaster Tools

To find many of the errors within your website you will need to login to your free Google Webmaster Tools account.

Login Screen

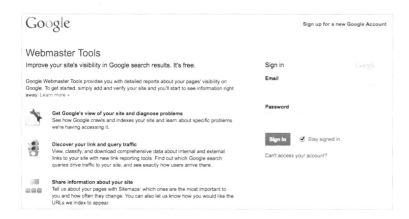

Don't forget

You will need to create, upload and verify an XML sitemap to fully unlock your free Google Webmaster Tools account.

Google's Webmaster Tools is a suite of tools supplied to help webmasters ensure that their websites are operating correctly.

This can be checked through the many available tools and services that include:

- General website overview

- Googlebot website view

- Sitemap checker

- Crawl analyzer and statistics

- Top search queries

- Site indexing statistics

- Linking analysis

- Robots.txt creation and analysis tools

- 404 pages enhancement tools

To really get the most out of this free tool and unlock all of its features you will need to create, upload and verify a sitemap which we will cover in Chapter 8.

Google Sitemaps

Hot tip

To learn how to create a sitemap and upload it to Google, see p104.

If you want to help yourself and at the same time help Google, then you need to get a Google sitemap.

Hot tip

Use Google sitemaps to identify the problem areas of your website.

Having a Google sitemap will offer you many great benefits. It will help you with:

- Understanding Google's view of your site

- Diagnosing potential problems with your website

- Seeing how Google crawls and indexes your website

- Monitoring the performance of your website

- Learning what search phrases bring traffic to your website

- Sharing information with Google to help it better index your website

This is one of Google's most useful tools. It enables you to tell Google when you have changed your website and what you have done to it. This means you will have more control over how quickly Google re-crawls your website after you make changes to it.

The other great feature is that Google will feed back to you crucial information about your website and its visitors, helping you further increase its effectiveness.

Google Analytics

If you would like to see how searchers are visiting your website, where they are coming from and how often they visit, then it's your lucky day. You can find out all of this and more by signing up to a free Google Analytics account, which gives you all the benefits of an advanced website statistics program.

Hot tip

Google Analytics can tell you exactly what your visitors are doing on your website, and it's free.

Signing up with the Google Analytics service will enable you to find out lots of information regarding your site and its visitors.

To sign up to Google Analytics for free just click Access Analytics and follow the steps below:

1 Log in using your Google account details

2 Click on the Sign Up button

3 Enter the website details and setting requirements requested and click Continue

Once you have signed up and installed the tracking code, Google will start to track your website and feed back valuable information that will enable you to optimize your site more effectively.

Linkdex

When you are optimizing websites, you can either do so manually or use specialist tools to help speed up the process.

Linkdex is a great example of a tool that can make the process of optimizing and analyzing your website much easier.

This software is available for free to website owners. There are no ongoing charges or fees to pay, making it an extremely useful tool for anybody seeking to conduct search engine optimization.

Premium versions are available, which enable you to carry out detailed link analysis on any site. Upgrading from a free account is easy, plus you will also enjoy one free month on signup.

Linkdex is jam-packed full of useful features including:

- SEO task and project manager

- Free keyword research suite

- Multi user facility to enable the outsourcing of tasks

- SEO reporting dashboard

- Free website optimization page scoring

- Multiple active projects

To register for this free tool and receive extra credits, visit the website at http://bit.ly/bennorman and follow the opposite instructions to set it up.

Set up your new account in Linkdex:

1 Select the Claim FREE Account link, then enter your detials and click Try Linkdex For Free

Start using Linkdex in 60 Seconds

Are you a business or a marketing agency?	Please select ⯆
What is your company name?	
In which country are you based?	Please select ⯆
What is your email address?	
What is your name?	
What password would you like?	
Please confirm your password	

☐ By clicking 'Try Linkdex For Free' you agree to the Terms of Service, Privacy, and Payment & Refund policies.

Try Linkdex For Free

Don't forget

You will only need to add your details once, as Linkdex will automatically remember them.

2 Enter a welcome code if you have one and click Next

Welcome to Linkdex

Linkdex is a free platform where you only pay for data that helps you measure and benchmark your online performance and create and complete more of the tasks that help you rank higher

If you have a code that gives you a guest pass to access our award winning data enter it here.

WelcomeData	No code. Don't worry, enter *WelcomeData*

Next

3 Enter the address of your website and click Next

Welcome to Linkdex

Your code allows you to rank, traffic and value check 100 keyword phrases weekly and check the backlinks of 4 domains.

Which domain would you like to promote first?

We call this a 'primary domain', and benchmark other websites' performance against it.

Next

4 Enter your main keywords and click Next

Welcome to Linkdex

Keyword Phrases ⓘ

List up to 100 keyword phrases you would like to rank for and the country you'd like us to check your rankings in.

✓ Rank check this domain in multiple countries
✓ Vary the frequency of checks from daily to weekly by keyword
✓ Tag keywords to create keyword groups
✓ Benchmark rankings, traffic and monetary value across multiple domains

Total Volume	132,895		
Total Media Value	$460,714		
Estimated Click Volume	35%	28,239	4,989	13,614
Estimated Click Share	0%	21%	4%	11%
Estimated Media Share	$1,795	$232,447	$36,473	$111,183

United Kingdom ⯆	

Next

Hot tip

If you are planning to use the free version, try to only enter your priority keywords so you don't use all your credits.

...cont'd

⑤ Enter phrases that define your market and click Next

⑥ Add a competitor's site to analyse and benchmark against your website and click Next

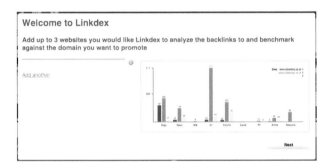

⑦ Congratulations, your new account has been created!

Now that you have successfully created your account, you will be able to use all of the tools that Linkdex offers.

This will save you valuable time as you do not have to enter your website details again.

Google Keyword Tool

As part of their ever-growing suite of tools, Google has its own free keyword tool that you are able to use to ensure you stay on the right track with your keyword research.

Although the tool is located under their AdWords section it is not only useful for managing and researching keywords for your paid search campaigns, it is also very useful for finding new keywords for use in the natural optimization of your website.

You will not get exact figures but more an indication of popularity and competition, which is very useful when deciding on which keywords to target.

There are two main ways in which you can use Google's keyword tool:

1. You can enter some seed keywords so that Google can elaborate and give you some other ideas

2. You can enter your web page address and Google will scan the content and advise you on what it thinks are the relevant keywords for your website

The best way is to use option one and, working one product/service at a time, enter in some relevant keywords and then see what is returned.

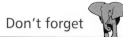

Don't forget

In the next chapter you will learn how to choose your keywords to enable you to get the most from the keyword research tools.

Wordtracker

Wordtracker is one of the most established keyword research platforms on the internet.

Wordtracker have a good free version of their premium paid keyword tool that you can use to gather search information for the top ten keyword results.

Although this free data does not include such information as competition figures, it does still provide you with a good indication of the most popular search phrases.

The premium Wordtracker tool is similar to the free version, except you can enjoy the following premium features:

- Save-to-basket feature to save sets of keywords

- Project manager for different sites

- Up to one thousand results per query rather than ten

- More search metrics to measure

- Ability to save Keyword Niches

- Access to Wordtracker's top one thousand reports

- Different search options such as misspellings

If you are going to be investing a lot of time and money into your website, or you have multiple websites, then it may well be worth investing in the premium version.

If you are only looking for a basic keyword tool to get an idea of keywords to target, then the free version should be adequate.

Hot tip

To get the free Wordtracker tool just Google "free Wordtracker".

Hot tip

To get a 10% discount on the paid version just signup via http://bit.ly/ben-norman-offer.

3 Choosing Your Keywords

Keywords are the phrases for which you want Google to display your website. It is important to ensure that the keywords you choose are both relevant and searched for. This chapter will explain how to choose and implement them.

Importance of Keywords

The most important part of optimizing your website is the selection and implementation of your keywords.

If you do not get this part of the optimization process right then everything else you do will be in vain. Target the right keywords and your website will be a success; target the wrong keywords and you will miss out on the valuable traffic you are trying to canvass.

Keywords are very important to your website because without them your website theme will not be focused and as a result it is more likely that you will not rank well in Google.

Keywords should be identified and incorporated throughout the whole design of your website so that you can ensure it is focused on targeting the ones you have chosen. This will ensure not only that your content stays on track and is more relevant to your searchers but also that Google can see how relevant your website is. This will greatly increase your chances of gaining high positions within Google for search phrases that will generate real traffic.

Google can only recognize your site as being relevant to your desired keywords if you have used them in your website and in the links you have pointing to your website. This may sound very simple but many websites seem to miss out the keywords they are trying to target.

Some of the most common mistakes made when targeting keywords are:

- Targeting stop words (see p40)

- Targeting keywords that are too broad

- Targeting too many keywords

- Targeting individual keywords

- Poorly representing keywords

- Not using different variations of keywords

Make sure that you do not make these common mistakes, as keyword selection is the foundation for your website's success within Google.

Using Multiple Keywords

Another common misconception in the selection of keywords is that when you are targeting them, you should only identify and choose single words.

This is wrong and if you make this mistake you will almost certainly be disappointed with your results. To get top placements for single keywords (other than company names) is very difficult and will often take years to achieve.

The correct way to choose and target keywords is to select multiple keywords together in a search phrase. A search phrase is made up of several words that are very relevant and make a search more specific.

Optimizing with search phrases has many benefits compared with using single keywords, including:

- Less competition for your search phrase

- A more relevant website

- Better chances of a higher position in Google

For example, if we were to build a website to sell this book we would target the keywords "Google Book" and "Google Books", as this would be much more relevant for our website than just targeting the keyword "Book" – and we would have cut our competition down substantially.

The other point to remember is that, although the broader keyword "Books" would get more traffic, it would not be as beneficial as you might expect it to be.

The simple reason is that if someone was interested in buying a "Google Book", that would be what they would search for, and through optimizing for that search phrase we would canvass the relevant traffic and not the irrelevant traffic.

The benefit of being specific is that we are only targeting relevant traffic. This is all we are interested in as this will more than likely convert into sales. The irrelevant traffic would probably only result in the selection of the Back button, which would be a wasted effort.

Hot tip

Using multiple keywords will dramatically cut your competition.

Don't forget

Keep your keywords focused to your website's theme.

Choosing Your Keywords

In order to choose your keywords, you need to have a rough idea of the terms you think will be relevant.

First, put together a list of the keywords you would expect people to type into the search engines when looking for your product or services.

When you have your basic list of keywords, it is time to bring in the reinforcements and put our new tools to work. It is always helpful to get a second opinion, and even a third, so we will use two different free keyword suggestion tools.

Wordtracker Keyword Tool

Don't forget

Keep your keywords relevant and within your niche.

1 Type "Wordtracker free" into the Google search box and click Google Search

2 Select the Wordtracker link

Hot tip

Don't just choose the keywords with the most traffic; look for keywords with low competition.

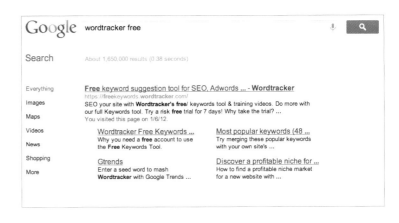

3 Enter your keyword phrase into the Keyword box and click Search

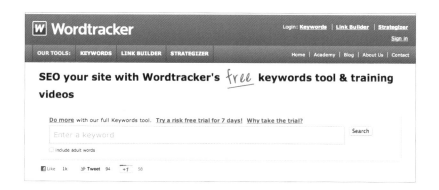

4 Your search results will be displayed as shown:

Be sure to record your selected keywords so that you have them for future reference and then move on to the next keyword or keyword variant.

You can always come back and review further keywords at a later stage as keyword research should be a continuous process.

Hot tip

Use your competition's keywords to give you ideas of where to start on your keyword search.

cont'd

Google Keyword Tool

To get started with this tool just follow the process below:

1 Type "google keyword tool" into the Google search box and click Google Search

Hot tip

Try to use multiple keywords to limit the number of returned results.

2 Select the Keyword Tool link

Google google keyword tool

Search   About 5,440,000 results (0.10 seconds)

Everything   **Keyword Tool - Google** Adwords
                https://adwords.google.com/select/KeywordToolExternal
Images   Enter one **keyword** or phrase per line to see what related word searches your ad will
                show on.
Maps

3 Type your keyword phrase(s) into the box and click the Search button

Your results will be generated as shown here. You can then evaluate these results to determine which keyword phrases will be most beneficial and relevant for your website

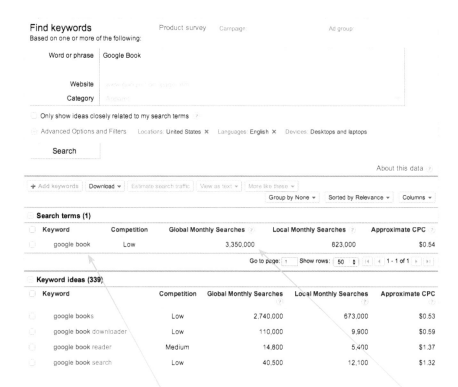

The keyword phrase that was searched for, including related searches

Number of searches conducted for keyword phrase

Now you have a new list of keywords. With the data you have collected from the two keyword suggestion tools, you are in a position to decide on the keywords to use.

The choice of what keywords to use is yours alone; but you must carefully weigh up not only the number of searches the keywords receive, but also how much competition there is for each of them.

Resist the temptation just to choose the keywords with the highest number of searches. Instead, focus on search phrases that are related and in your niche, as this will make top placements easier to achieve.

Don't forget

Ensure that all of your keywords stay relevant to your website's theme.

Don't Copy, be Unique

When you are trying to decide on what keywords to choose, it can seem an easy option just to copy your competition.

This would be a big mistake, as most of the time this is what your competitors have also done.

The worst part of it is that your competition may well be targeting the wrong keywords themselves, because they have not performed their own keyword research.

Too many people are just copying each other and taking it for granted that the keywords must be right because everyone else is using them.

The other problem that you will most likely find when you assess your competitors' keywords is that they will be targeting lots of single keywords. This, as we know, is a big mistake and it will help you to identify the competitors that are not targeting effective keywords.

This is not to say that you should ignore the keywords your competition are using, as to do this could lead to you missing some good ones.

The knowledge gained from assessing your competitors' keywords will help you get a better idea of those you need to check and evaluate.

Some of these may prove to be relevant enough to use or they may even open the door to some new keywords you had not thought of using.

Copying your competitors' keywords without doing any other research, however, will cause you several problems including:

- More competition
- Unknown effectiveness of keywords
- Missing out on more effective keywords
- Lack of relevance to your website theme

Finding more unique keywords to target rather than just copying your competition will increase your chances of gaining a higher position on Google.

Beware

Don't just copy your competitors' keywords, because if you do you will have no idea of what traffic you will receive and how relevant it will be.

Find Your Niche

The best and easiest way to top Google's listings, as we already know, is through having the most relevant site.

There is an easy way to help your website achieve this level of relevance. The way to be really effective is to find your niche and become the authority on it.

Many website owners try to optimize their websites for too many search phrases so that they simply spread themselves too thin and end up achieving nothing.

Most websites start off small with a limited number of pages. Instead of starting out with a small selection of finely tuned keywords, they try to rush in with every keyword they can think of and there is just not enough related content to make it effective.

For example, for "Google Book" all of our search phrases will be related to this search phrase. If we were to copy most website owners with our keyword selection we would be targeting all types of broad search phrases such as:

- Book

- Internet Book

- Search Engine Book

- SEO Book

We want to keep our website within a niche so we would be targeting keywords such as:

- Google Book

- Google Optimization Book

- Search Engine Optimization for Google

- Google SEO Book

Doing this will help keep our website theme very specific and Google will be in a much better position to see the true relevance of the site.

If we had followed the other method, we would have diluted our website theme and we would not be deemed as relevant.

Hot tip

Creating a niche website will increase your relevance and make optimizing your site easier.

Don't Use Stop Words

It is important when you are choosing keywords and search phrases that you do not use or include any stop words.

Stop words are words that Google considers to be irrelevant to its search results and so it ignores them.

These insignificant, frequently occurring words include:

Beware

Using stop words within your keywords will dilute their relevance.

40

- And
- A
- The
- In
- On
- Of
- Be
- I
- Me

Stop words will dilute the weighting of your keywords and search phrases and this is why it is important not to include them.

Google's algorithm will ignore these stop words as they are deemed to be unnecessary and only serve to slow down the process of assessing your website.

This does not mean that you shouldn't include them in your website itself – you should. It would read very strangely if you left them out.

You should use stop words in your body text but you should try to refrain from using them in your:

- Meta titles
- Meta keywords
- Links
- Header tags

Long Tail Keywords

When looking at the subject of keyword research it is impossible to avoid the mention of long tail keywords.

Long tail keywords are similar to your main keywords with the exception that they are phrases of typically three words or longer.

The longer and more specific a search query is, the less people will target it so there is less competition.

For example, in marketing this book a main phrase would be "Google book". But focusing on the long tail keywords we would use such phrases as:

- SEO book for Google

- Book on optimizing my site for Google

- Getting to the top of Google book

The downside of using long tail keywords is that they do not generate the high volume of traffic you would see from keywords such as "book" or "Google book".

There are many benefits to using long tail keywords as part of your keyword strategy, including:

- Less competition

- Higher conversion rate

- More relevance to your website

- Quicker to rank

- Higher initial ranking position

- Lower bounce rate

The main benefit of using long tail keywords is that they are easier to rank for.

If you have a relatively new website, then starting with some targeted long tail keyword phrases is the best place to begin.

You won't get large amounts of traffic but the traffic that you do get will be more relevant and more likely to convert.

Hot tip

If you have a new website then using long tail keywords will make getting a top position on Google much easier.

Common Mistakes

When it comes to choosing keywords and implementing them to your website, there are a few common mistakes that are often made such as:

- Choosing vanity phrases
- Copying competitors' keywords
- Trying to target every keyword possible
- Picking keywords purely on search volume
- Only implementing keywords to the home page
- Using the same keywords on every page
- Overusing keywords in page copy
- Using phrases that are not relevant to the website
- Targeting one phrase throughout the whole website

One of the main mistakes that people make is to get caught up chasing vanity phrases such as "book" when really this is making their job more difficult.

Vanity phrases are less relevant and there is much more competition. This means that you will end up doing a lot more work for a lot less reward.

To ensure you do not fall into this trap ask yourself the following five questions when selecting keywords:

- Is the competition for this phrase unrealistically high?
- Is this phrase really relevant for my website?
- Are these keywords really the most relevant for this page?
- Is there enough search volume?
- Can I imagine people truly searching for this?

If you follow the above you should avoid the common pitfalls when it comes to selecting and implementing your website's keywords.

Beware

Search volume is never exact and the results can sometimes get distorted so always ask yourself: "Can I see someone searching for this?"

42

Keyword Selection

When you are researching your keywords to decide which ones you are going to use, just follow the steps below:

1. Navigate to your keyword tool of choice

2. Enter in any relevant phrases for your website and generate the results table

3. Working down the list, pick out any relevant phrases including long tail keywords and record them

4. From your results, split the keywords so that each of them is under the page of your website that it is most relevant to

5. Page by page work through the keywords and decide which ones are most relevant for that page

Beware

If you don't pick relevant keywords for your website to target, your content will not make sense.

Selecting which keywords you are going to use within your website should not be rushed as it is arguably the most important part of the optimization process.

When selecting your keywords remember:

- No vanity phrases

- Pick the most relevant phrases

- Don't pick based purely on search volume

- Use long tail keywords

When choosing multiple keyword phrases to target on the same page it is important to think about how you are going to represent them on that page.

This means that you really need to ensure your keywords stay focused, otherwise your pages will not make sense to your visitors and they will not convert.

Using Keywords Effectively

Once you have spent the time researching and gathering your keywords, you need to ensure that you represent those keywords throughout the different pages within your website.

To make sure you get the most value from your keywords they need to be represented well within your:

- Meta descriptions
- Meta keywords
- Page titles
- Alt tags
- Header tags
- Body text
- Link anchor text
- Website navigation
- Page names
- File names

It is also very important where, within the different fields, you place your keywords. This comes down to two main factors:

Keyword Prominence

Keyword prominence refers to how close a keyword is to the start of a particular field.

It is deemed that the closer a keyword is to the start of a field the more important that keyword is.

Keyword Density

Keyword density refers to the amount of times a keyword appears in a particular field (often referred to as a keyword's weight).

It is important that your keywords have a good prominence and density and this is why you should not target too many phrases on any one page.

Hot tip

When writing content, ensure you use your keywords as many websites don't.

44

Beware

Do not overuse your keywords or your website may be labelled as spam.

4 Know Your Competition

Your online competition can hold the key to your success. Through careful analysis you can utilize their strengths and avoid their weaknesses.

Who is Your Competition?

One of the most important things when optimizing your website is to know your enemy.

Your competition hold the answers to how to get to the top of Google. You just need to know what to look for and how to analyze the data you find.

To know how to find your competition you must first have identified the keywords that you wish to target and found the sites that rank among the top results.

It is important to remember that your online and offline competitors are not necessarily the same. Your online competitors are those sites which appear in the top returned results for the same search phrases your own potential customers are using.

To identify your online competition, take your list of keywords and for each of them search Google. You should take note of the first 20 returned results and record these websites as they will be your online competitors.

Hot tip

To find your main online competitor, look for the site that is frequently in the top of the search results for the majority of your search phrases.

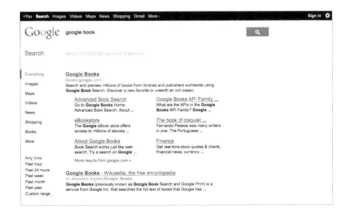

Once you have done this for your list of keywords it's time to analyze the results.

If you have got the keyword selection process correct you should find a correlation between the results; you'll see that the websites returned are normally very similar each time. You will usually find that one website will be in every set of returned results and this site is likely to be the most correctly optimized of the group and most relevant in Google's eyes. It is also likely to end up being your main online competitor.

What Keywords do They Use?

Now you have identified who your competition is, it's time to look behind the scenes and see what keywords they are targeting.

To do this we are simply going to look at the HTML code of the website as Google would see it. This is perfectly acceptable and does not involve hacking into websites or any such illegal acts.

To look at the code just navigate to the required page, right-click on it as shown below and select View Source. This will then open up a new page of text.

Hot tip

You can also view the source code by selecting Source from your browser's View toolbar.

47

Source code

```
<!DOCTYPE html PUBLIC "-//W3C//DTD XHTML 1.0 Strict//EN" "http://www.w3.org/TR/xhtml1/DTD/xhtml1-strict.dtd">
<html xmlns="http://www.w3.org/1999/xhtml" xml:lang="en">
<head>
<meta http-equiv="Content-Type" content="text/html; charset=iso-8859-1" />
<title>In Easy Steps: Homepage</title>
<meta name="description" content="Computer Step is the leading computer books publisher,the world's favorite compu
<meta name="keywords" content="computer books, internet books, in easy steps, computer book publisher,">
<link rel="stylesheet" type="text/css" href="./css/master.css" />
<!--[if lt IE 7]>
<link href="/css/iesucks.css" rel="stylesheet" type="text/css" media="screen" />
<![endif]-->
<!--[if IE 7]>
<link href="/css/ie7sucks.css" rel="stylesheet" type="text/css" media="screen" />
<![endif]--><script type="text/javascript" src="./js/scripts.js"></script>
<script src="http://www.google-analytics.com/urchin.js" type="text/javascript">
</script>
<script type="text/javascript">
_uacct = "UA-457659-6";
urchinTracker();
</script>
</head>

<body>
        <div class="skipper">
            <span style="display: none;"><a href="http://www.richardquickdesign.com">web Design Cornwall</a>.<
        </div>
        <div class="wrapper">
            <div class="top-nav">
                <form id="search_form" method="post" action="./search/" onsubmit="return searchCheck('sear
            <div class="top-nav-search">
```

Don't forget

If your competition is only using single keywords, they are not making full use of their website and are not correctly optimized.

Now that we can see the page as Google sees it, we can pick out the important Meta information to see what keywords are being targeted. We need to single out the three main areas of information that we are going to use to identify the keywords.

...cont'd

Meta tags

Meta Title   Meta Description

Meta Keywords

The Meta information is made up of three main parts:

- Title – This is displayed in the top of the browser to identify the page

- Keywords – The main words and phrases users search on, hopefully to find your site.

- Description – This is the description of the web page, to be displayed in the search results. (It is important to remember that Google does not use this description as it will create its own from the content of the page. Google still analyzes this tag and other search engines use it, so it should still be incorporated.)

You should note the keywords used as you can assess these and decide whether you can or should be targeting them.

If the website is optimized, you will notice that some of the keywords will also appear in the description and title tags. These will be the main targeted keywords and you should note them down.

If you cannot find a correlation between the results of the different searches, it means that the websites are not optimized effectively and this will make things easier for you.

48

Who do They Have Links From?

Now we know what keywords your competitors are targeting it is time to see who links to them. This may sound impossible to find out but with the Google toolbar it is made easy for you.

With your list of competitors' websites to hand, go to their home pages. Right-click on a page and navigate to Page Info, then select Backward Links.

This will then take you to Google, and waiting there will be a list of web pages that include a link to that page:

Don't forget

You can also check backward links by navigating to the home page and selecting the Backward Links option from the PageRank section of the Google toolbar.

You now know every web page that links to your competitors' websites and that Google rates. This information will prove priceless in the linking section. It will enable you to look to these sites to gain links into your own website, as you know who is interested in linking to sites like yours.

Competitor Positions

Your competitors will be in the positions they are in for one main reason. Google believes their websites to be the most relevant for the search term queried.

Google will have arrived at this decision by running the websites through its algorithm. It will have found your online competition to be most relevant for those keywords, by analyzing and finding them and similar words in their:

- Meta title
- Meta description
- Meta keywords
- Alt tags
- Header tags
- Main body of text
- Bold or highlighted areas
- Internal links
- External links

Google will also have looked at links on other people's web pages pointing to these websites, and analyzed the following points:

- Quality of the site the link is on
- Link anchor text (text in the links pointing to the website)
- Relevance of the link (is it on a similar site?)
- PageRank of the page the link is on
- Number of other links on the page

All of these factors and more will contribute to your competitors' search engine placements. It is through the analysis of this data that it is possible to find out why they are in the positions they are in.

Once you know what they have done, it makes it easier to create your action plan for achieving a higher position for your website.

50

How Optimized are They?

To see what you need to achieve for your website, it is useful to see how well optimized a competitor's website is compared with yours. To do this there is a good free tool for the Google Chrome browser called SEO Site Tools.

To download the tool, first make sure you have downloaded the Google Chrome Browser and then follow the below instructions.

Hot tip

Get the Google Chrome browser free from www. google.com/chrome.

1 Google "SEO Site Tools", and click on the link

2 Click the "ADD TO CHROME" button which installs the plugin in your toolbar

Hot tip

Ensure your website is more relevant than your competitor's to achieve higher positions in Google.

3 You will now see the new SEO Site Tools button in your Google Chrome toolbar

...cont'd

Hot tip

To get some really good data on your competitors' link profiles use the Linkdex tool.

4. Navigate to a website you would like to compare to and click on the SEO Site Tools Button. You will then see a results window detailing the link profile of the checked website. From this window you will be able to see what links they have and where they are coming from

5. If you now select the "Page Elements" tab, you can review the on page details and see how well optimized their website is

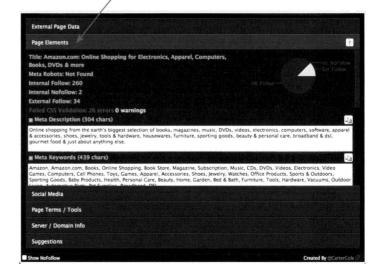

6 · If you now select the "Social Media" tab, you can review how active they are on the various social media platforms

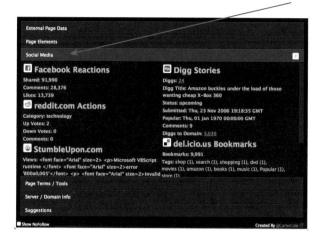

7 · Finally, if you select the Server / Domain Info tab you can review their domain age and hosting information

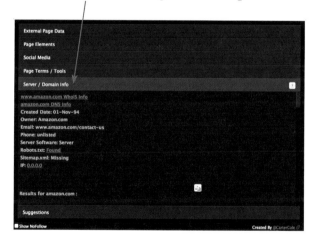

SEO Site Tools is a feature-rich tool for analyzing your competitors' websites. It will show you what they are doing and what you are doing differently.

This information will enable you to spot the weaknesses in your competition and ensure your website does not suffer from the same problems as theirs.

How to Top the Competition

To top your competition and achieve a higher position in Google, you need to make Google see your website as more relevant than your competitors' sites.

This can sometimes seem like a monumental task but it can, over time, be achieved as long as you stick to Google's rules and work on increasing your relevance.

The first step is to analyze your competition and evaluate their websites to determine their strengths and weaknesses. Once you have done this it will help you to work out your plan of attack. You will be utilizing their strengths and learning from them. You will also need to learn from their mistakes and weaknesses, and use these to give your website the upper hand.

There are three areas that you need to focus on for your optimization and these are crucial for gaining the edge over your competition:

- New relevant content creation – This is where you will create new content to help build the relevance of the site with Google, and further help your website visitors

- On-the-page optimization – The optimization of your website. This is where you will make sure that it is targeted only to relevant keywords that will help to focus your chosen theme

- Off-the-page optimization – This is where you will work on increasing your inward links and securing a higher PageRank for your website than the competition have for theirs

If you concentrate on optimizing these three areas then you will be increasing the relevance of your website not just for your visitors but also for Google.

Over time, as Google re-crawls your website and sees it gaining in relevance as the new changes are introduced, Google's view on your website will become more positive.

This is the only way to achieve higher positions in Google's natural search. This, unfortunately, takes time to achieve but it is worth it in the long term. If you keep increasing the relevance of your website, you will keep improving your position.

Beware

If your competitors are doing something that does not look right, do not just follow suit. Use the forums (see p204) to make sure it is ethical.

5 Setting up Your Website

The setting up of your website is one of the key parts of your optimization. If you get this part right, you will save yourself a tremendous amount of time and trouble in the future. This chapter will help walk you through the process and avoid some of the major pitfalls.

Domain Name Choice

The choice of your domain name can help with the optimization of your website, as the name can be used to inform the search engines about the relevance of your site.

The first thing that your domain name will tell Google is what geographical area your website is targeting. For example, if you are using a .com name, it is more likely that your site will be based in the USA, whereas a .co.uk domain would be located in the UK.

This is not to say that you cannot use another domain extension. It is just easier to have your site identified correctly if you use the most appropriate extension for your country.

Example domain extensions and locations are:

- .com – US company

- .co.uk – UK company

- .net – US network

- .ca – Canadian website

- .de – German website

The second thing your domain name can tell Google is how relevant your website is to your subject area. For example, if your site had the domain name www.google-books.com this would probably be because it was relevant to the content and so at a guess you would sell or have something to do with "Google books". Also as it is a .com it is likely that you are US-based.

It is important to remember that if you have a domain that is not relevant to what your website is about or your extension is not exactly what it should be, Google will tell in time but there can be confusion in the beginning until Google gathers enough information about your website to identify it correctly.

Don't forget

Use the domain extension that is relevant to your location.

Hot tip

Try to use your keywords in your domain name if possible to increase your relevance.

http://www.ineasysteps.com

Domain name

Extension

Domain name age is an important factor when it comes to optimizing your website for Google.

Google views older domains as being more established and less likely to be spamming.

The problem is if you do not already have a domain with some age on its side you need to get one and start from square one. Right? Wrong, if you would like to get a domain name with some age on its side you can get one but it will cost you a little bit more depending on how old it is, what Page Rank and how many links it has.

You can buy domains from many places online but one of my favorites is Sitepoint (http://www.sitepointmarket.com):

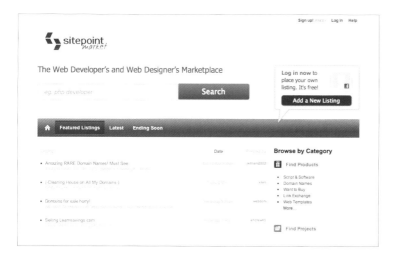

They have various different auctions and "buy it now" is where you can purchase aged domains that are no longer required. You can even purchase websites that have been set up but are no longer required, to save yourself even more time.

To ensure you get a good domain name you need to check the following:

- The domain has Page Rank

- The domain has some links

- The domain is the age they say it is

Hot tip

To check a domains age you can navigate to www.123-reg.co.uk and search for the website. Click on the taken link and it will tell you when it was registered and by whom.

Hosting

The hosting of your website is a very important service and you should always do your research before you sign up.

Google can use the location where your website is hosted to determine the country your website is targeting.

This can sometimes cause unnecessary problems when you have hosted your website in a country other than the one you are located in and which you are targeting.

Hot tip

When choosing a hosting provider try to go on recommendations or ask relevant forums for advice.

For example, if you have a UK-based website for your UK-based company but you are using a .com domain extension, and you are also hosting your website in the USA, it could be very easy for Google to assume you are actually based in the USA.

This could prove difficult because you would not be shown in UK-specific searches (those that specifically target sites in the UK) and you would miss out on your most relevant traffic.

Normally when you are choosing your hosting, your decision will be based on cost alone. But there are many options you should consider before you sign up, including:

- Cost

- Location of the servers

- Uptime of the servers

- Ease of contact with the provider

- Technology supported and supplied

- Platform of the hosting (Linux or Windows)

- Bandwidth

- Webspace

The uptime of your hosting provider is a very important factor that you should take into consideration when making your decision.

Some service providers will now offer 100% uptime, which means that they will ensure your website is online and available 100% of the time.

This is a great benefit to you as the last thing you want when people choose to visit your website is to find they can not access it for technical reasons.

If Google tries to visit your website and it is not consistently available, it cannot be confident that your site is reliable.

You may find that if your website is often down, Google may not rank it highly or may even remove it from the search results.

When assessing which type of hosting you require it is important to always have in mind what the purpose of your website actually is and what market you are in.

If you have a five-page brochure website only to give you a presence online then the chances are that you only need a very basic package.

If you have a website that is your business i.e. the majority of your business is done online, then your hosting is much more important.

You should ensure you invest wisely and seek out a more reliable and professional web host to ensure that you are not only online all the time but if something goes wrong you have a dedicated support team available to put the problem right. I have always found Rackspace to be very good if you want to ensure your website stays online.

When it comes to hosting, you'll find that bigger is normally better. Larger, well-established web hosts will have greater capacity to ensure that in the event of hardware failure, their backup systems will kick in and prevent your website from going down.

To ensure you get a good web host make sure they have:

- Guaranteed uptime

- Proven disaster recovery plan with timings

- 24/7 support by phone

- Supported server side software and upgrades

- Good reviews across the Internet

Beware

Do not choose an unknown provider that you cannot contact easily just because it is the cheapest.

Validation and Accessibility

The way in which your website is designed and built is a key factor in achieving higher positions in Google.

If your site's code is put together correctly this can help give you an advantage. It provides several benefits, including:

- Enabling Google to crawl your website more easily
- Reducing the risk of errors when the site is crawled
- Being more accessible to searchers and search engines
- Conforming to the W3C guidelines

Accessibility is an important issue on the internet and you need to make sure that you take this into account when you build your website or have one built. It is important to test your site to ensure that it has taken these things into consideration.

The W3C is an important committee that was set up to help with accessibility of web pages to all users on the internet.

Since 1994 it has been publishing the standards and guidelines to help ensure the web reaches its true potential.

Tests for accessibility can be found on the World Wide Web Consortium website at www.w3.org. Depending on the technology used to develop your website, you will need to use the appropriate test.

If your website validates, you will be able to use the official W3C badge on every page. This is a good thing to display as it will show that you have taken these factors into consideration and that your website is accessible.

If your website fails to be validated, the testing tool will give you a list of reasons why, and you will then be able to rectify them and retest it.

Please note that for the example on the next page we will be using the HTML validator link as our website is in HTML, but you should substitute a different version for your website's technology if necessary.

To see if your web page validates, please follow the steps opposite:

Hot tip

If you are having a website built, always make sure it validates before you sign it off.

Beware

If your website does not validate you could be discriminating against people by not allowing them to access your material.

1 Google "W3C" and navigate to validator link

2 Enter your website address into the box and click Check

W3C Markup Validation Service
Check the markup (HTML, XHTML, ...) of Web documents

Validate by URI   Validate by File Upload   Validate by Direct Input

Validate by URI
Validate a document online:

Address: [   ]

▸ More Options

                    Check

This validator checks the markup validity of Web documents in HTML, XHTML, SMIL, MathML, etc. If you wish to validate specific content such as RSS/Atom feeds or CSS stylesheets, MobileOK content, or to find broken links, there are other validators and tools available.

W3C Markup Validation Service
Check the markup (HTML, XHTML, ...) of Web documents

Jump To: Validation Output   Congratulations · Icons

This document was successfully checked as HTML 4.01 Transitional!

Result:	Passed
Address :	http://www.ben-norman.co.uk/
Encoding :	iso-8859-1
Doctype :	HTML 4.01 Transitional
Root Element:	HTML

The validator will then come back and tell you if the website has passed or failed. If it does fail, you will be given a clear indication as to why so you can rectify it.

Page and File Names

Page names are the names of the specific pages on your website. A page name identifies and separates that page from others on your site.

http://www.ineasysteps.com/books.htm

Page name

Hot tip

Use your keywords in page names and file names where relevant.

Page names should be used properly and optimized so that they can assist Google in deciding what your pages are about and determining their relevance. They will help Google to decide the relevance of each page both in terms of your website theme and whether it should show the page in its results.

To optimize your page names and file names you simply need to know what keywords you are trying to target for each page and try to use them in the page names and file names where relevant. It is important to remember that you should not just cram keywords in; your purpose is to add relevance, not to mislead.

For our Google book website we would try to use relevant page and file names with our keywords included. So for our About page we would not use the name /aboutus.htm as this does not help increase our relevance or tell Google what the page is about.

Beware

Do not use your keywords excessively in each file name as this would be spamming.

We would instead use (depending on the keywords we had chosen for the page) /about-google-book.htm as this allows us to build in much more relevance.

Not only have we helped Google by telling it what the page is about, we have increased our relevance and helped optimize our page by including our keywords in the name.

This can be used for every page on the website and, if used properly, it can give you the edge over your competition.

You cannot use spaces in file names. If you wish to separate words you can do so by using – or _. This will ensure they are seen and interpreted by Google as separate words as it will see those characters as spaces.

It is very easy to change your page names if you have a static website but it can sometimes be more tricky if you have a dynamic website.

If you have a static website you simply need to edit the page name, which in most website publishing programs can be done by simply selecting the page and choosing the Edit option.

Most design packages, including Dreamweaver, will ask you whether you wish to automatically update your links, and for this you would select Yes.

This feature will ensure that all of the links that point to the old page name will now point to the new one. This is a particularly useful feature and will save you lots of time now and avoid lots of problems in the future.

If you have a dynamic site you will need to contact your webmaster or the company that deals with your content management system (CMS) to discuss whether it is possible to customize the page names.

Your webmaster may then be able to implement a facility that will enable you to name your own pages. Once this is implemented you will be able to edit your page names using your current content management system.

Next and most importantly you must put in place a 301 redirect, which will tell the search engines that the page has been renamed permanently and that they should update their records to reflect this. See the next page to learn how to do this.

If you are creating a new website you do not need to worry about this, but if you are editing an existing website you must ensure you do it or you could end up with dead links and this will mean that traffic doesn't get to you.

Implementing a 301 redirect will ensure that any traffic going to the old page will now be redirected to the new page and ensure that your PageRank is transferred.

It is always worth getting your page names and file names correct at the outset so that you do not have to worry about implementing 301 redirects later.

Hot tip

Dreamweaver will update your links automatically for you, saving you time and avoiding problems.

Redirects

Redirects are essential in the updating or changing of a website and must be used correctly. There are a few different types of redirect but we will only be concentrating on one type, the 301 redirect.

The 301 redirect is the most search-engine-friendly way to redirect traffic from one page to another. The 301 simply tells Google that you have moved a page permanently and where you have moved it to. This then enables Google to update its records and pass on any PageRank that may be attached to the page.

You should use a 301 redirect if you want to:

- Change a page's filename

- Move a page to another location on your website

- Move your whole website to another server

To implement a 301 redirect is very easy to do. Here are the methods for the three most common technologies:

301 Redirect for pages using a .htaccess file on a Linux server

Open up your existing .htaccess file using Notepad. (If one is not available, create a Notepad page named .htaccess)

Insert the following line into the file:

redirect 301 /oldfolder/olddomain.htm http://www.yourdomain. com/newfolder.htm

(To add more pages just duplicate this on new lines.)

Now change the relevant parts of the code to reflect your own website and page details.

Save the file and upload it to the root folder of your server, and you're done.

If you wanted to redirect a whole website you would just replace the line with:

redirect 301 / http://www.yourdomain.com/

Hot tip

Using a 301 redirect will make sure that Google knows your page has moved. It will pass on the PageRank to the new page.

301 Redirect for pages using asp (Windows Active Server Pages) on a Windows server

Delete all of the code from the old page and replace it with the following, substituting the names of your own domain and page:

```
<%@ Language=VBScript %>

<%

Response.Status="301 Moved Permanently"

Response.AddHeader "Location", "http://www.yourwebsite.com/
newpage.asp"

%>
```

Beware

If you use the wrong redirect it will not work correctly.

301 Redirect for pages using asp.net (Windows Active Server Pages) on a Windows server

Delete all of the code from the old page and replace it with the following, substituting the names of your own domain and page.

```
<script runat="server">

private void Page_Load(object sender, System.EventArgs e)

{

Response.Status = "301 Moved Permanently";

Response.AddHeader("Location","http://www.yourwebsite.com/
newpage.asp");

}

</script>
```

Once you have implemented your redirect you should navigate to the old page to make sure that it is redirecting correctly. This is imperative as you do not wish to lose traffic through dead links and missing pages.

You should also check whether you have any back links for the old page, and if so have the relevant sites update their records to point to the new page.

Hot tip

If your required redirect is not given here, use Google to find it.

Cascading Style Sheets

Cascading Style Sheets, (more commonly known as CSS) provides a very useful technology when it comes to creating your website.

Using CSS will give you many great benefits including:

- Complete control over the appearance of your website

- Site-wide changes by just editing one sheet

- Separation of the design and the content of your site

- Faster page downloads for your visitors

The main benefit when it comes to using CSS on your website is that it allows you to keep its content separate from its structure. This makes for higher content weighting, which helps your site increase its relevance.

CSS is also very useful to Google as it does not have to go through everything and can just assess the content of your website, which is the part Google is interested in. Also, because you are keeping up with technology, Google will view your website more favorably.

Using CSS can make the difference between Google having to go through this (a page without CSS):

Hot tip

CSS will help keep your keyword weighting high.

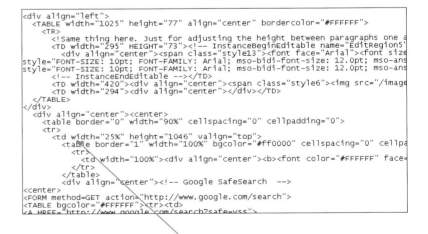

Structure on page with content

...or this (with CSS implemented):

```
<div class="wrapper">
    <div class="top-nav">
        <form id="search_form" method="post" action="./search/" o
<div class="top-nav-search">
    <label for="search_box" class="hide">Search</label>
    <input type="text" name="search_string" id="search_box" value="Se
    <input type="image" src="./images/button_go.gif" alt="Go" />
    <input type="hidden" name="search_loc" value="ALL" />
    <input type="hidden" value="AND" name="search_type" />
</div>

        <div class="top-nav-lnks-holder">
            <ul class="link-list">
                <li><a href="./" class="lnk-wdth-1 on">hoi
                <li><a href="./books/" class="lnk-wdth-2"
                <li><a href="./company/" class="lnk-wdth-
                <li><a href="./resources/" class="lnk-wdt
                <li><a href="./company/contact/" class="l
            </ul>
        </div>
    </div>
    <div class="breadcrumb">
        <h1 class="hide">Homepage</h1>
    </div>
    <div id="content">

        <div class="col-1">

            <div class="home-main-panel" style="background-im
```

Content linked externally

Don't forget

Always check that your CSS validates to the W3C standards. See p60-61.

As you can see, using CSS is a very effective way of controlling the layout of your website.

It is also good because it enables you to separate the formatting code from the actual content so there is less for the search engines to have to crawl to find the content

You should also remember if you are using CSS to ensure that it validates by using the CSS Validator on the W3C website.

1. Navigate to the CSS Validator

2. Enter your website address into the box and click the Check button

3. If the CSS does not validate then you will need to correct the problems and then re-validate

For more information on CSS and how you can make it work for you, see **"CSS In Easy Steps"**.

67

Dynamic Sites and Pages

Dynamic websites are very common these days, especially for shops with a large number of products, and other sites with many pages of information. They can pose some problems with the optimization process but you can also turn this complex system around to work for you.

Dynamic websites use standard template pages that are populated from a database. This makes the information easier to store and manage.

The database structure can be a great help in your optimization campaign because, with some fine tuning, you can make it do some of the hard work for you.

For example, if you have a large database of products and you wish to optimize the Meta titles for their pages (and each Meta title needs to be the same as the product name) you could do this dynamically.

You could set up the database to input the product name into the page title for every page on your website. This alone could save you weeks and would mean you only needed to input this data once.

You could then use a similar rule for the description Meta tag, using the first line of the description of the product to populate it. This is one of the benefits of a good content management system.

If you are having a dynamic website built or are looking to buy an off-the-shelf package, be sure to ask the following questions to ensure the package will give you every chance of being able to optimize your website fully:

- Will I be able to choose and change my own page names?

- Will I be able to change the Meta information on each page?

- Will my pages validate and conform to the W3C rules?

- Will I be able to input Alt tags for my images?

- Will I be able to input heading tags?

Ensuring that your new dynamic site conforms to the above will save you time now and problems in the future.

Hot tip

Talk with your webmaster to see how your dynamic site can make the optimization of your website easier.

Beware

If you purchase a cheap content management system with no upgrade facility you will limit how much you can optimize your website.

Avoiding Frames

It is very important to keep up with technology on the internet and make sure your website is current and moving with the times. This means avoiding using old and outdated technology that will work against your efforts to achieve a high placement in Google. It is therefore important to avoid using frame-based websites.

Using frames was a very popular option for creating websites in the early years. This has now become a very unpopular option as frames keep all of the details of your website off the page. This means that Google cannot *see* what we can *see*.

What we see:

What Google sees:

```
<html>
<head>
<!-- url = http://www.oscarenterprises.f2s.com/ -->
<meta http-equiv="Content-Type" content="text/html; charset=iso-8859-1"><tit
<frameset rows="100%,*" border="0" framespacing="0" frameborder="0">
<frame src="http://www.oscarenterprises.f2s.com/">
</frameset>
<noframes>
<body>
The website for britishbarbecue.co.uk can be found by clicking <a href="http
britishbarbecue.co.uk is registered through <a href="http://easily.co.uk">Ea
</noframes>
</html>
```

What we can see and what Google can see are very different and Google is unable to assess any of the content because it is hidden. This means that Google is totally reliant, when assessing websites that use frames, on the Meta information and inward links.

This is not a good situation to be in. If you have a website that uses frames it would be in your best interests to transfer it over to a newer technology.

Beware

Using frames will work against your optimization efforts.

Beware

Having a totally Flash-based website will put you in the same situation as having frames. Google will struggle to index such sites properly, so stick to Flash images, not entire Flash sites.

Do's and Don'ts

Setting up your website is a very crucial stage and should not be rushed.

Your website is going to be your online salesperson to the world and should properly and ethically represent your company.

This is why it is important that your website gives out the right message.

If you put the effort into your website at this early stage and get it right it will pay dividends in the future and make optimizing your site easier and more effective.

When setting up your website, use the checklist below to ensure you are on the right track and not making silly mistakes:

When creating your website do:

- Use CSS
- Choose the right domain name and extension
- Ensure it validates before signing it off
- Host it in your own country
- Use redirects correctly
- Use a logical and optimized structure

When creating your website do not:

- Use old technology such as frames
- Go for the cheapest option
- Use non-customizable dynamic sites
- Rush and throw it together
- Hide text with keywords in it on the page

This is a very simple checklist but if you ensure you follow it, you will be saving yourself time and avoiding major problems further down the line.

Beware

Do not accept second best from your web designer. Ensure you are happy before signing off the project.

Don't forget

Time spent now will ensure you do not have to redesign the site again in the near future.

Breadcrumb Trail

A breadcrumb trail is a series of text links moving from left to right that show visitors where in a website they are, and gives them a fast and easy way of navigating back to any of the previous pages.

Breadcrumb trail

Beware

Do not just stuff keywords into your breadcrumb trail; it must be relevant to the linked-to page – and make sense.

Breadcrumbs are a vital part of the design of your website as they will help with the website's overall:

- Usability

- Search engine optimization

The reason breadcrumb trails are so valuable from a search engine optimization standpoint is that you are able to use your keywords in the anchor text and link through to the most valuable page.

This increases the weighting of your chosen keywords within your internal linking profile which in turn helps to indicate the relevance of your website to the search engines.

When using breadcrumbs remember to:

- Use your keywords in the breadcrumb links

- Structure it with the homepage on the left

- Ensure all your links go to the right place

A breadcrumb trail is a very valuable part of your website's navigation so ensure that you don't miss it out of your website build.

Blogging

A blog is an online journal that people use like a diary to provide commentary or news on a particular subject.

Blogs are becoming more and more common on the internet as they are a great way of keeping a record that everyone can access.

These can be very useful if you wish to keep people up to date with what is going on. You can even allow people to comment or add their own entries to your blog.

Blogs are a great way for businesses of all sizes to communicate with both existing and future customers.

By having a current blog about your niche subject you can generate large amounts of related content over time. Google, of course, feeds on good content.

Websites that are constantly updated with new and valuable content will be crawled by Google more often than those that are not. Yours will therefore be deemed a more relevant resource than a competing website which is out of date.

The end result for this is normally a higher placement on Google and more traffic.

If you would like to create a blog for your website you have two options:

- Use an external blog solution

- Install your own blog software

You can get an external blog via sites like www.blogger.com, which you set up like a web-based mail account.

Hot tip

Having a blog will increase your website's content and relevance as long as you keep it related to your website's theme.

Don't forget

You need to ensure that your blog stays topical and relevant.

72

Alternatively, you can download free blog software from
www.wordpress.org and set it up on your web server so that you
have total control over it.

To download this free software just follow these steps:

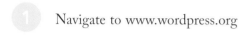 Navigate to www.wordpress.org

 Select the Download link

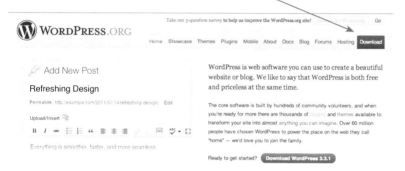

Click
Download
WordPress

Click OK
to start
downloading
the software

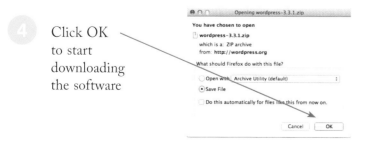

RSS Feeds

RSS or Really Simple Syndication to give it its full name, has really changed the way in which people can keep up to date on the internet.

RSS feeds make it easier than ever to get in touch with those people who are interested in what you have to say.

In the old days if you wanted to stay in touch with people you would have to rely on email and telephone.

Now people are working smarter and when they find resources they would like to keep up to date with, they can bookmark their RSS feeds and have fresh content delivered to their RSS feed reader as soon as it is put online.

If you have a blogging platform such as WordPress attached to your website then the chances are it will have an RSS feature built in and will keep itself updated.

This means that all people will need to do is click on the orange feed button on your website and they will be able to bookmark it. In the future any new content added will be delivered straight to their feed reader.

If you would like to start following some RSS feeds to keep yourself up to date then the Google reader is a good place to start.

You can download the Google reader for free at http://www. google.com/reader as part of your Google account.

Hot tip

Make sure your website's RSS feed is picked up by the main search engines by navigating to http:// pingomatic.com and submitting it.

6 Designing for Google

When creating your pages it is possible to satisfy both your website's visitors and Google. This chapter will help optimize your site's content so visitors are greeted with compelling copy and Google places you favorably within its search results.

Searchers Not Search Engines

When optimizing your website content, it is crucial to remember who will be reading it.

First and foremost you are writing your content for your human visitors.

Achieving a high position in Google is irrelevant if your copy does not read well. All of your efforts will be in vain because people will not be able to read and understand it.

This having been said, if you construct your pages properly you can easily satisfy both your human visitors and Google's search engine spiders. To do this you need to ensure that you do not get side-tracked with the creation of your content and you keep it specific and relevant.

It is easy just to litter your pages with keywords and hope for the best, but there are several problems with this approach:

- Google's algorithm can tell this is what you are doing

- Your copy will not be easy to read

- Your website will not convert its searchers so well

- Your website will not be as relevant as it could be

The main problem is that even if this trick worked, when searchers got to your page they would not hang around for very long.

People don't expect to have to read through keyword-stuffed pages to find what they want. Searchers expect to find what they want in a logical, easy-to-digest order.

This makes the construction of your pages crucial, so ensure you get the most from them by:

- Ensuring they are structured to inform on a personal level

- Ensuring the content delivers benefits to your readers

- Ensuring you use your keywords and other semantically similar words

- Using header tags where appropriate

Beware

If you forget about your human visitors when you create your content your efforts will be in vain.

Be Unique

You should always ensure that your website's copy is unique and not duplicated anywhere else on the internet. This means that each of your own pages should be one of a kind, not exactly the same as others with a few words changed here and there.

Your web pages should all be relevant to your site's theme and you should use them to target different keywords. Each page is unique and you should target that page to canvass certain keywords. It is worth noting that not all of your visitors will enter your website through your home page. If one of your deeper, more specific pages is more relevant to the searcher's query, they will be taken directly to that page.

Google has a complex and sophisticated algorithm that is more than capable of spotting duplicated work. If it finds this, the pages will not be added to its database and they will be ignored. This would totally defeat the object of having created them in the first place. It is also worth noting that you should not, in any case, copy content from other websites and duplicate it without the website owner's written consent.

Google checks for duplication for several reasons including:

- Ensuring search results are delivered quickly

- Keeping the results relevant

- Avoiding duplicated results

- Preventing copy theft

The main reason Google checks this is to ensure that its search results will always be relevant and delivered as quickly as possible. After all, if we were to query Google with a search phrase and it delivered thousands of pages with exactly the same content it would be of little use to us.

There are times when your copy will need to be the same as that on another website if it is factual or a record of some sort. You can get around this by:

- Linking to the other page instead of copying the text

- Writing the page in your own words and laying it out differently

Beware

If you use text copied from another site on your page, Google will not add your page to its database.

Website Theme

Every website should have a theme so that Google can tell what it is about.

The theme is determined by assessing all of the pages of the website to establish what they have in common.

This theme should always:

- Express the niche you have chosen for your website
- Include your main keywords

This is why it is so important to have a good structure, as this will make it easier to define your website theme.

To ensure your website theme is well defined you should ensure that your main keywords are included in the:

- Meta title
- Meta description
- Meta keywords
- Alt tags
- Header tags

To make this effective, you should mix in your keywords with other relevant words for the individual pages. So for our Google book we would probably have something like the following page names:

- /google-book.htm
- /about-google-book.htm
- /google-optimization-book.htm
- /website-optimization-google.htm
- /google-seo.htm

This would ensure that our main keyword "Google Book" is seen as being very relevant to our website theme. By using other relevant words as well we not only make it more natural but we are also canvassing them as search terms, increasing our possibility of being found from other targeted search phrases.

Hot tip

A niche website theme will help you achieve better positions.

Don't forget

Ensure your keywords are linked into your website theme.

Content is King

When it comes to getting your website listed on Google, there is one thing that can make or break your chances more than anything else. Yes, you've guessed it: the content!

The content on your website is the key element that will separate your site from all of the others on the internet.

Great content will:

- Increase your chances of Google finding you relevant and placing you in a good position

- Increase the likelihood of other websites in your industry linking to you

Content is what Google hungers for and it is always looking for new and more relevant content to show in its results.

If you have a website full of good content and you keep it up to date and add to it regularly, Google can tell. Google will then look to your website more often and visit it more frequently.

Every website in every industry can have good, useful and unique content. You can create useful content by incorporating:

- Relevant help pages

- Information pages

- Calculators

- Tips and cheats pages

- A relevant blog

- A free forum

Google will derive the majority of its information on page relevance from your content - it is this and this alone that will secure top placements. Without quality content on your website you really have nothing to market and your website will be of little use to your visitors.

If you have good and unique content you will start to find that people are linking to your website, which in turn helps your page optimization.

Beware

If you do not have relevant content, your website will never succeed in Google.

Hot tip

Ensure you know what keywords you want to target with your page before writing it, as this will help you use the keywords throughout your page.

Don't forget

Good, relevant content is what Google is looking for so make sure it can be found on your site.

Header Tags

Header tags are very important when it comes to optimizing your web pages and they need to be used sparingly, as their misuse or overuse will not work in your favor.

The six header tags

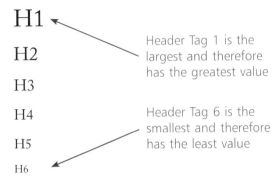

H1 — Header Tag 1 is the largest and therefore has the greatest value

H2

H3

H4 — Header Tag 6 is the smallest and therefore has the least value

H5

H6

The <h1> tag, as it marks the largest text, holds the most weight and importance with Google.

The <h6> tag marks the smallest headers and is considered the least important.

This is not to say that you should make all of your header tags <h1>, as that would look silly and also water down the importance of them all. The header tags should be used to help lay out your pages, with the main title being an <h1> tag and the next being <h2>, etc.

You should always try to use your main keywords for the page in your header tags along with the title and main content as this will increase their relevance.

Normally the header tags will appear at set sizes that may not fit in with your website's design but that is not a problem. You can set up a new cascading style sheet and set the sizes in that so that it will overrule the header tags' normal size, making the page look more balanced.

Alt Tags

Alt tags are the descriptions of the images used on your website.

These simple tags enable your website to be more accessible to all – including Google. Alt tags are a necessity on every website that uses images for three main reasons:

- They make your site accessible

- They enable screen readers to interpret your images

- They enable Google to interpret your images

Many websites still do not use Alt tags correctly. They are not only breaking accessibility rules but are also limiting their positions on Google.

Hot tip

Alt tags will show the relevance of your images to Google.

How we see images:

How Google and screen readers see images:

This is what the screen readers see when viewing the images

```
<a href="./resources/"><img src="./images/home/panel_re
alt="Resource center: Downloads articles and more" /></
```

If you don't use the Alt tag, Google and the screen readers have no idea what that image is trying to convey – which benefits no one. If you take the time to populate the Alt tag with a relevant description, however, your images will be much more accessible.

If you do this everyone benefits (including you) because the more you describe your images, the more relevance you will build into your website – and Google will recognize this.

The other benefit is that more people can access and use your website so the chance of conversions increases.

Beware

If you do not include Alt tags in your website it will not validate.

Structure Your Page

Reasons to structure your website

- Keep things organized

- Help build your website theme

- Build in more relevance to your search strings

- Help Google crawl your website more effectively

- Make expanding your website easier

To add some structure to your website we would need to create some folders and move the pages to their relevant folders.

Remember to ensure that you update any links and set up redirects to the new pages to ensure you have no dead links. This will also ensure that the PageRank you have is passed on to the relevant new pages.

Content with no hierarchical order

- Index
- Who wrote the Google Book
- Who Published the Google Book
- How much is the Google Book
- Example of Google Book
- Ease of use
- Optimizing for Google
- Contact google book

Don't forget

Structure your website properly and you will make your life easier.

Note how all of the pages sit in one place with no hierarchical structure.

This means that you would be missing out on valuable opportunities to build in relevance to your website.

Each page would be given a shorter URL because a possibly optimized folder name would not be included. You would miss out on the chance to create more relevance.

Content in a hierarchical order

- Index
- About Google Book
  - Who wrote the Google Book
  - Who Published the Google Book
  - How much is the Google Book
- How Google Book Works
  - Example of Google Book
  - Ease of use
  - Optimizing for Google
- Contact google book

Note how all of the pages sit in their own relevant folders with a hierarchical structure. There is an order present to help identify where each page sits.

A further benefit is the way the web address will be displayed to increase the relevance, and you can optimize the folder names to build in even more relevance. For example, instead of calling the services page folder of your website /services, why not be more specific? If you provide financial services why not call the folder that? This all helps Google see the relevance of your website and rank you accordingly.

Unstructured URL

No optimized folder or page name included

http://www.ineasysteps.com/?9781840783322

Structured URL

http://www.ineasysteps.com/computer-books/google-book.htm

Includes the optimized folder and page name

The structured site has a longer URL for each page but it is more logical, it contains our keywords and it gives Google more information as to what the page is about.

Meta Tags

Meta tags are important things to get right on your website, as they will be telling Google what your site is about and helping it build an accurate website theme.

They will also be used to describe your website in the search results.

There are many different types of Meta tags but we will only be concentrating on the three main kinds:

- Meta title

- Meta description

- Meta keywords

This is how the three Meta tags look in the page source (please note that they should always be placed between the <head> and </head> tags):

Meta title

Meta description

Meta keywords

```
<meta http-equiv="Content-Type" content="text/html; charset=iso-8859-1"
<title>In Easy Steps: Homepage</title>
<Meta name="Description" content="Computer Step is the leading computer
<Meta name="Keywords" content="computer books, internet books, in easy s
<link rel="stylesheet" type="text/css" href="./css/master.css" />
```

The first and most important Meta tag is the Meta title tag, which is used and displayed at the top of the browser window and also in the title of Google's returned result for your page.

The second Meta tag is the Meta description tag, which is used and displayed in the description for your page in other search engine results. Google looks at this tag but it will display its own description, picked from your page, that is most relevant for the searcher's specific query.

The third Meta tag is the Meta keywords tag, which is where you can list the keywords that you feel would be relevant for your page. Google now places very little weighting on this tag as it has been so much abused, but it is still worth having as some of the other search engines will use it.

Page Titles

The page title is the most important tag that you will be using, as it describes the page.

We talk about the title tag as being part of the Meta data when officially it is not, but for convenience we will include it with the Meta information.

Each page should have its own title that is not only unique and descriptive but also chosen to take into account the keywords for which you are optimizing the page.

The title tag will be displayed both in Google's natural listings in the search engine and also at the top of the browser window to identify the page.

Page titles in action

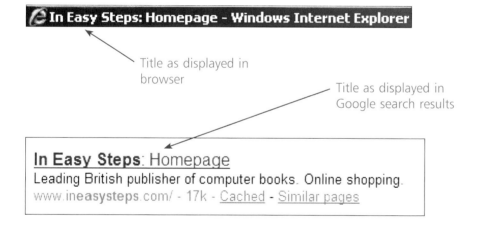

Title as displayed in browser

Title as displayed in Google search results

The Meta title tag should always come directly after the opening <head> tag so that it is found first.

To create the perfect title remember to:

- Include your main keywords

- Keep it page-specific

- Ensure it is in keeping with your website theme

- Keep it short and focused

Beware

Do not use the same title for every page.

Don't forget

Ensure the title tag is the first tag in your <head></head> section.

Meta Description

The second Meta tag is the Meta description tag.

The Meta description tag is used to describe your website to searchers looking at your site's result in the search engines.

Google looks at this tag but it will display its own description, picked from your page. Google will display a snippet of your content that it believes to be most relevant for the searcher's query.

Although Google does not display this information, it will read and assess it and so it is still important to get it right.

In Easy Steps: Homepage
Leading British publisher of computer books. Online shopping.
www.ineasysteps.com/ - 17k - Cached - Similar pages

Description as displayed
in Google

Meta description

```
<head>
<meta http-equiv="Content-Type" content="text/html; charset=iso-8859-1"
<title>In Easy Steps: Homepage</title>
<Meta name="Description" content="Computer Step is the leading computer
<Meta name="Keywords" content="computer books, internet books, in easy
<link rel="stylesheet" type="text/css" href="./css/master.css" />
<!--[if lt IE 7]>
<link href="/css/iesucks.css" rel="stylesheet" type="text/css" media="s
<![endif]
```

Creating the perfect description

- Include your main keywords

- Keep it page-specific

- Ensure it is in keeping with your website theme

- Keep it short and focused

- Avoid repeating your keywords over and over

- Write it to be read, not for use with the keywords tag

Meta Keywords

The third Meta tag is the Meta keywords tag.

The Meta keywords tag allows you to input the keywords that you feel are most relevant to your page – the ones for which you wish your page to appear when Google is queried.

Meta keywords

Beware

You will not achieve high placements just by placing your keywords in the Meta keywords tag.

Google no longer places great weight on this tag as it has been so much abused in the past but it is still worth having.

This is because it is still likely that Google will look at the keywords here, and some of the other search engines will still use them.

This tag can also be useful for variations of words that you have not used. For example:

- Abbreviations of your keywords
- Semantically similar words
- Incorrectly spelt alternatives of your keywords
- Plurals of your keywords

Hot tip

Use the keywords tag to target semantically similar and incorrectly spelt keywords.

It is very important to note that just because you put a word in your keywords, your page will not necessarily appear for that term.

If you have not mentioned the word in your content and you put it into the keywords tag, you are really just wasting your time.

Many people new to optimization believe this tag to be the be-all and end-all of optimizing a website, when really it is not.

Remember when using this tag to use search phrases, not just single words.

Use Your Keywords

Use your keywords throughout your pages to ensure you get the most from them.

For some reason when people create a website they tend to forget to use their keywords. This is a big mistake because if you do not use them Google is not going to be able to see their relevance. This means that you are not going to appear in search results or rank well for them.

Your keywords should be used through your entire website, not just on one keyword-strewn page. Each page should have its own specific keywords and be named appropriately to help target them further.

Google uses something called "Latent Semantic Indexing" (LSI), which is a technology within its algorithm. This technology examines the words on your website and can determine whether they are semantically close to each other.

When people write they will naturally use different words that mean the same thing; for example, the following words are semantically close:

- Search engine optimisation

- Search engine optimization

- SEO

- Organic SEO

Google would know that these words are similar and so using them all would add more relevance to your website.

If Google finds that your website is only using one keyword over and over again it can decide your site is unnatural-looking and you may not rank as highly as a result.

You should also consider this when building inward links as this will ensure that your links look more natural. It is always better to vary the anchor text in the links so that it looks more natural.

If Google believes that your website is gaining links naturally, it will be looked upon more favorably and this will add more weight to your links and the keywords they use.

Hot tip

Do not just use your keywords – use different abbreviations and semantically similar words and phrases.

Beware

If you do not use your keywords in your content Google will not be able to see the relevance of your website.

Body Text

Body text, otherwise known as web copy, is the main text on your website and is where the bulk of your main content will be placed.

Web copy should be:

- Compelling

- Leading

- Unique

- Around 500 words or less

- On topic and focused (no rambling)

- Well written and free from grammatical errors and typos

- Optimized for the keywords the page is targeting

Beware

Poor web copy is one of the quickest ways to lose visitors to your website.

Your website copy is arguably the most important part of your website when it comes to getting it right.

It is all well and good getting visitors to your website but if the copy is not compelling and well structured you will never be able to convert them.

Good web copy will take a visitor and lead them through your website, informing and filling them with confidence at every step of the way.

To ensure you get your copy right just follow the steps below:

1. Ensure you have researched the keywords to target

2. Understand the message you are trying to convey and the desired action you would like the visitor to take

3. Plan where you will put the links, which page(s) they need to go with and the anchor text you will use

4. Write the page taking into account the above points

5. When happy with your copy be sure to thoroughly check it to ensure it is free from errors

Nofollows

Nofollowed links were introduced by Google as an instruction to the search engine not to follow certain links.

A normal followed link looks like this:

<a href="link.htm">linked page<a/>

A nofollow link looks like this:

<a href="link.htm" rel="nofollow">linked page<a/>

When you set a link to be nofollowed this is what happens:

- Google won't follow the link
- Page value is not passed to that page
- Anchor text relevance is not passed across to that page

Using the nofollow tag is a great way to stop PageRank and relevance from being passed to pages where it is not required.

For example if you were linking out to many of your suppliers to build credibility, you may not want to pass on PageRank so you could nofollow those links.

The nofollow attribute was previously used in an attempt to influence the value a page was given by the search engines. However recently its has discounted and therefore no longer plays as big a part as it may have done previously.

You should use nofollows when:

- You are linking to sources you may not trust
- You link to generic pages such as Contact Us and Terms and Conditions pages
- You don't want to pass on page value to a certain page

7 Optimizing Your Website

Optimizing your website is the key to ensuring that Google can see the true relevance of what you are offering.

Beware

Google takes more into account now than just your Meta data, so ensure your content reflects this.

How it Was

In the early days, website promotion within the search engines was a much easier process than it is now.

The search engines used to rely purely on what the website owner said about the site. This meant that to optimize your website you only had to rely on your page optimization.

A website owner just needed to submit their site to the various search engines they wanted it to appear on.

The search engine would then send its spider to crawl the website and would store it in its cache so that it could be analyzed and then ranked.

The search engine would analyze a website based on the information the website owner had given in the Meta tags.

To optimize your website you simply needed to place the keywords for which you wanted to appear in the Meta tags, and that was about it.

People soon realized that if they used a specific keyword in their Meta keywords tag more frequently than a competitor did, they would appear higher than that competitor.

This meant that to appear at the top of the search engines for your keyword you had to have it in your Meta keywords tag more times than anyone else.

For example, if you put the keyword in your Meta keywords tag 10 times and your nearest competitor put it in 11 times, you would be second and they would be first.

To get into first position you would put it in your site 12 times. This spiraled out of control and caused the Meta keywords tag to lose its value. More complex algorithms were brought in to make the search results more relevant.

This way of assessing a website, based purely on the website owner telling the search engine what the site was about, was very much open to manipulation.

This offered no benefit to the searcher as the websites you were shown in your results often had no real correlation with what you originally searched for.

How it is Now

The way search was going, something had to change to ensure that it remained relevant.

Because of the abuse the Meta tags were receiving, the results that would be shown for your queried search could end up being totally irrelevant.

The search engines had to combat this, and they put in place more criteria against which to assess websites. This was when the Meta keywords tag was given less importance, and less relevance weighting was placed on it.

The search engines started checking more points in their algorithms to ensure that websites were truly relevant, including:

- Meta tags
- Domain names
- Header tags
- Bold text
- Keyword weighting
- Keyword prominence
- Alt tags
- File names
- Link anchor text

A major innovation was the use of off-the-page factors, which involved the analysis of what other sites said about yours.

Another important factor that has helped make search more relevant is Google's PageRank algorithm. This algorithm assesses the links that come into your website from others and judges how relevant and important those links are.

This has enabled Google to add a very important criterion when analyzing websites for relevance: how other people describe your website. This is a very useful tool, as other sites are less likely to be misleading and will give a truer representation of what your website is about than you would.

Hot tip

Utilize your inward link text to ensure that other sites increase your site's perceived relevance.

Don't Optimize for Your Domain Name

One common mistake often made by website owners is to optimize their sites for their domain names and/or site names.

This is a big mistake for several reasons:

- Your domain name is unique to you

- The site name will be represented throughout your site

- Your company name will be well represented naturally within your website

- You will dilute the other keywords you are using

The main way people misuse their domain names is to put them in every Meta title on every page before the keywords for which they are really trying to optimize, and this causes several problems, including:

- Reducing the weight of your keywords

- Reducing the prominence of your keywords

- Detracting from your website's theme

In Easy Steps: Homepage - Windows Internet Explorer

Now by removing the domain name from the title tag and adding in some of your keywords, you will still rank for your domain name but you will increase the weighting and prominence of all of the other words in your title tag.

Computer Books - Windows Internet Explorer

The above title tag is now set up to help target our main keywords and will help with our optimization and the task of adding relevance to the website.

If you ensure that you do not optimize for your domain and company name, you will make optimizing for your desired keywords much easier.

Hot tip

Remove your site name from your titles to increase your rankings for the other keywords.

Beware

Optimizing for your domain name will reduce the weight of your other keywords.

Analyzing Your Website

If you would like to assess your website pages and see how well optimized for Google they are, there are a couple of simple ways to check them for free.

You can either use the Site Optimization tool for Google Chrome, alternatively you can use the free tool that you registered for earlier from Linkdex.

Either tool will allow you to assess the keywords you are using and show how well represented they are within your website as a whole, as well as on individual pages.

This will enable you to make sure that the keywords are well represented and that you stand a good chance of having a page that Google will find relevant.

Whilst you can analyze the page yourself, Linkdex will be able to provide a much clearer insight in a significantly reduced timeframe.

The software analyzes the top sites and works out what Google is looking for, based on the keyword representation throughout the site. As a result it can assess how close your website is to being the best.

You can also use SEO Site Tools to review the individual pages of a website and the various elements in evidence on each. This can be particularly useful to quickly check how well optimized a web page is.

Hot tip

Ensure that you analyze new pages before putting them live on your website, in case you need to change them.

Elements to analyze:

- Meta title and description

- Header tags

- Alt tags

- Internal link anchor text

- Keyword use page copy

- W3C validation

- File names

How to analyze your website with Linkdex

...cont'd

 1 Open Linkdex and select the Site Optimization tab

2 Click the Optimization Score link

3 Review the scores for each section and note down any changes required

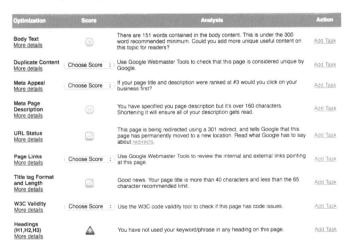

4 You can then review each page of the website in turn to identify any possible issues

How to analyze your website with SEO Site Tools

1 Navigate to your desired website page and click the SEO Site Tools button

2 Select the Page Elements tab and review the various elements are relevant and contain the correct keywords

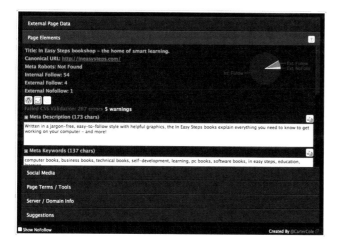

3 Review desired pages and ensure that each one is targeting a relevant keyword and that all fields are populated correctly

Optimizing Your Website

Now that you have analyzed your web pages, you will have generated a list of actions that you need to perform so that your page is fully optimized.

It is important that your website is as close to this as you can get it, as it will then be in line with the top sites for your selected keywords.

One of the easiest ways to work through the changes that are required is by using Linkdex.

You can also make things even easier by using their built in task manager to schedule and assign tasks to others.

Optimize your pages using Linkdex

Beware

Do not compromise the content of your website by just inserting keywords to reach the limits suggested.

1. Open Linkdex

2. Navigate to the Site Optimization tab

3. Review the points one by one

4. Decide what you need to change and update

5. Implement changes to your web page, ensuring that you are keeping true to your website's theme and that you avoid spamming (see p99)

6. When you have done this, run the report again and check that the result is now in line with what is required

7. Move on to the next point and repeat the process

Hot tip

Try to ensure that your website is within the limits specified, to maximize your on-the-page optimization.

It is important to remember that you should never just sprinkle keywords here, there and everywhere, as this will not help you.

You should always ensure that your page stays true to what it is representing, and you will find by doing this that you are fairly well optimized.

Spamming

Spamming is a big issue on the internet and you should ensure that you do what you can to avoid being responsible for spamming Google.

Spamming is when you deliberately try to mislead the search engines into including your web pages in their search results. This is done by using several different methods and tricks, including but not limited to:

- Creating keyword-littered pages
- Excessive keyword repetition
- Hiding keywords on your page
- Using extremely small text
- Duplicated content
- Doorway pages (see p208)
- Link farms (see p209)
- Cloaking (see p207)
- Keyword stacking (repeating the same keywords with variations in the case of the letters)
- Hidden links
- Typo spam (see p210)

If you notice a website that is utilizing these or other spamming techniques, you can report it to Google using the following link:

http://www.google.com/contact/spamreport.html

Benefits of reporting a spamming website to Google

Google will investigate a website that you report for spamming and may then:

- Remove the site from its listings
- Blacklist the domain
- Use the information to help make its algorithm better

Beware

Get caught spamming and you face having your site blacklisted and removed from Google's search results.

Do's and Don'ts

Optimizing your website is essential to enable it to be found on the internet.

If you follow the simple rules below you will ensure you have done what you can to optimize your website correctly. You will also avoid doing anything that could potentially harm your website's ranking within Google:

Do

- Ensure that you include your keywords in your Meta tags
- Ensure your file names and folders include your keywords
- Use a logical and optimized structure
- Use your keywords in your Alt tags
- Use your keywords throughout your content

Don't

- Keep repeating keywords in your Meta data or content
- Use misleading Meta data that is not related to your content
- Hide text on the page
- Have all pages in one folder
- Duplicate content
- Neglect to validate your pages

This is a very simple list but if you follow it you will avoid nasty penalties for spamming and misleading Google.

Don't risk Google's penalties

If you break the rules you could find:

- Your website blacklisted
- Your website sandboxed (see p205)
- A reduction in your position
- Your website removed from Google's results

8 Let Google Know You are There

Submitting Your Website

One way to let Google know your website exists is to submit it to the search engine yourself.

Submitting your website is a way of telling Google that it is there and asking Google to assess it for inclusion in its search results.

It is important to note that you need to submit your website to Google once and only once. It has been claimed that constant submission to the search engines will help your position in their search results, but this is not true.

Website submission is simply a way of telling the search engines that your site is there.

Although you do not need to submit your website to get indexed in Google's search results, you can manually submit.

Submitting manually to Google

Hot tip

Submit your website only when you are happy with it. This means that when Google first looks at it, it will be at its most relevant.

1 Google "add url to Google"

2 Enter your websites URL and the captcha

Don't forget

Google will find your website through its links so submission is only a precaution.

3 Select "Submit Request"

Linking into Google

One sure way to get into Google's listings and make sure it knows you are there is via linking.

If you have just one link into your website from another site that is crawled by Google, then Google will find you without you having to do a thing.

If you have no links into your website there is no connection, and the only way Google will know that you are there will be for you to tell it by submitting your website. This process could take a long time if Google has many sites already in its queue waiting to be crawled.

Having links pointing at your website is a much easier and faster way to have your site crawled.

Google finds your website through other links by sending its spider out to crawl the internet. The spider will find out the current results so that it can update its search results to ensure they stay up-to-date and relevant.

If you have a link from one of the websites crawled then the Googlebot (the spider) will find your site through that link.

Google will then index your website and consider showing it within its search results for those phrases which it considers relevant.

The extra benefit with this method is that through creating links into your website, you will also be helping to optimize your off-the-page factors (see p209). If you have optimized inward links, then you are also increasing your website's relevance and the chance of a good position for your optimized keywords. See the next chapter for more information about this.

These factors will all work together to get Google to notice your website and will give your site the opportunity to be included in its search results.

Optimized inward links will also help increase your PageRank, which is another major factor that Google uses when assessing the relevance of websites for keywords.

Creating Your Sitemap

Once you have your Google account activated (see p22), you just need to create your sitemap and upload it. To achieve this, follow the instructions below:

1 Navigate to www.sitemapspal.com and enter your domain name in the box

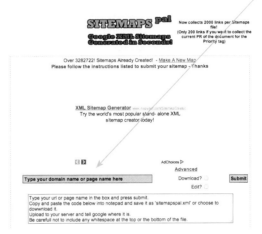

2 Check the Download box and click Submit

3 The information in the red box needs to be downloaded and saved as a new text file named sitemap.xml

4 This sitemap.xml file must now be uploaded to the root folder of your website on your server before you can submit it to Google

Google Sitemap Submission

Now you have created your sitemap you need to log in to your Google account and let Google know it is there.

To sign up to Google Sitemaps and upload yours, follow the steps below. (Ensure that you have uploaded your sitemap to your webserver root folder as /sitemap.xml before you start this process.)

1 Sign in to your Google account and select the Webmaster Tools link from the main menu

2 Select your website from the list

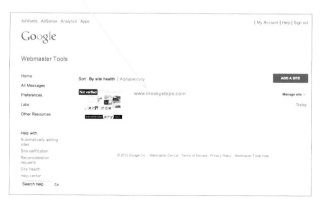

...cont'd

3 Click the Submit a Sitemap option

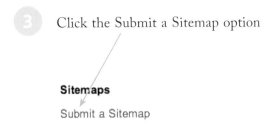

Sitemaps

Submit a Sitemap

4 Enter the address of your sitemap and click Submit Sitemap

Submit a Sitemap to tell Google about pages on your site we might not otherwise discover.

Submit a Sitemap		Show submissions: **By me (0)** - All (0)
www.ineasysteps.com/		Submit Sitemap	URLs in web index

5 Google will now queue your website to be crawled

Google will have added your sitemap to its crawl list and will soon visit your website and start feeding back information.

It is a good idea to check back after one to two days to ensure that your Google sitemap has indeed been crawled and that there have been no problems with the process.

Occasionally you will find that there has been an error while crawling your sitemap and you may need to repeat the process.

Google will report back if it experiences a problem and detail what the error entailed, so you can correct it.

As with anything, it is imperative that you keep your Google sitemap up-to-date. To do this you can just repeat the steps on the preceding pages to re-create and re-submit your sitemap.

Beware

There is no point having a Google sitemap if you do not keep it up to date and relevant.

9 Linking to Your Success

One of the most effective ways to achieve great results with Google is to create good quality links to your website. These links are important, but even more so are the source sites and the text within the links. In this chapter you will learn about the links you need and the links to avoid.

Why Links are Important

Hot tip

Good inward links will greatly increase your chances of good positioning.

In Google's mission to make search more relevant it will utilize all the information it can find about your website. This includes the information it finds in your incoming links.

Inward links help Google determine:

- What your website is about

- Which keywords are relevant to your site

- How important your site is

- Where your site is located

Google will utilize this information to assess where it should place your website in its results. This place will of course depend on how relevant your website is deemed to be for the particular search term queried.

Google gives great weight to what other websites are saying about your site. This has proved to make search more relevant and the results displayed more helpful to the searcher.

This is because other websites are more likely to be impartial and truthful about your website than you would be.

This is why when you evaluate a website you can find that it ranks very highly for a search term never really mentioned in it. If you then check the back links for such a website you will most likely find that it has many relevant sites linking to it using specific keywords as the link anchor text.

Google relies on what other websites are saying about your website for your off-the-page optimization. This includes:

- What anchor text is used

- The theme of the website the link is on

- The theme of the page the link is on

- The PageRank of the website the link is on

PageRank

To evaluate web pages properly, Google uses its PageRank algorithm.

This complex algorithm is used to determine how important web pages are, based on the links they have coming into them, and of course the value of those links.

PageRank displayed in the SEO Site Tools toolbar

← → C ⓘ ineasysteps.com   ☆ 🔍 ⚒

To see the PageRank of a web page, navigate to that page and review the number displayed by SEO Site Tools

Hot tip

When looking for inward links check to ensure the linking site has a good PageRank.

Google counts each link into your website as a vote from that website for yours, and likewise if you link to another site, that would be counted as a vote for that site. This is a very simple explanation, as the algorithm will take into account much more than just the number of links you have coming into your website.

Google also takes into account many other factors, including but not limited to:

- Quantity of links

- Relevance of each link

- Text in the links

- The PageRank of the sites you have got the links from

- The importance of the sites you received the links from

- Whether the links are one-way or reciprocated

Authoritative websites have a higher PageRank. If you get one relevant link from an important site, it could well be the equivalent of a thousand non-relevant links.

Google uses sophisticated text-matching techniques to ensure that it knows just how relevant your links are. These techniques tell it what every website, including yours, is about. If your links come from websites that match yours, this is of greater importance than if there is no relevance involved.

Types of Link

There are four types of link, but only three that we are going to be concentrating on.

The inward link

This is the most important type of link when it comes to optimizing your website as it will really help you increase your site's relevance and PageRank. An inward link is simply one that someone else creates from their website to yours. You do not have to link back to their site.

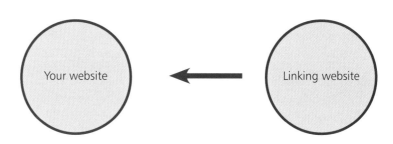

The external link

This link can be used to help build relevance for your website by linking it to other relevant sites. This is useful if it will help the people who are visiting your website.

If you do not trust a site or want to pass on link value you can always nofollow your external links.

I would always recommend having some followed external links as not doing so would look very unnatural. Also, if a website is really worth linking to then you should try and leave it followed so Google picks it up and gives it the reward it deserves.

Hot tip

Try to get mainly inward links as this will help to improve your PageRank faster.

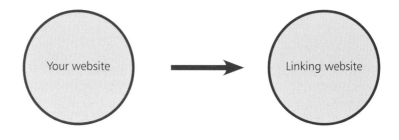

The reciprocal link

This type of link is normally used as a trade where one site will link to another on the condition that they link back. This can still be useful but only if the website is relevant to yours and will be of value to your website's visitors.

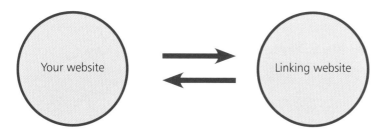

The three-way link

This type of link is normally used with the sole purpose of misleading the search engines.

Because reciprocal links have been devalued, webmasters now try to use three-way links as a means of generating a link without the correlation between just two websites.

As with everything designed to trick the search engines, it will eventually get picked up and you could find your website penalized so in my opinion it is best to avoid them.

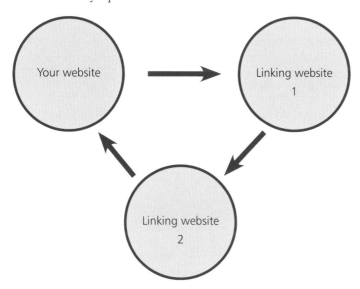

Beware

Do not take part in link campaigns aimed to trick Google as eventually you will get found out and your website will most likely be penalized.

Deep Links

Deep linking is the practice of creating a link which goes directly to a page other than the home page.

A normal incoming link looks like this:

http://www.ineasysteps.com

A deep link looks like this:

http://www.ineasysteps.com/books/

Hot tip

If you get a few relevant and keyword-rich deep links to some of your child pages you will see them start to climb the rankings.

When you are link building you should aim to get at least 20% of your links as deep links.

The reason deep links are so good is that they go straight to the most relevant page on your website and if you can get the anchor text really specific for that page, it makes your chances of a top position for that page even more likely.

Ways that you can encourage deep linking are:

- Ensure the page has very strong, unique content
- Promote the deep page as a resource in its own right
- Have a deep linking policy
- Have deep links that people can cut and paste on the links page of your website
- Actively ask for deep links instead of home page links

Deep links can be harder to get as many places such as directories will only link to your homepage, but there are a few good ways to obtain them, including:

- Press releases
- Articles
- Forums

112

Spamming

Spamming is a serious problem on the internet. You must always be aware of what you are doing and ensure that your activities are not spamming in any way.

Spamming can have serious effects on your website including:

- Giving it a bad name
- Associating you with dubious websites
- Giving your company a bad name
- Losing your relevance
- Making you very unpopular

Link building can sometimes seem a very tiring task and it can often be tempting to use one of the many automated alternatives available on the web.

This is not a good option as they actually just spam your link to various sites that do not want it and will simply remove it, including:

- Blogs
- Forums
- Guestbooks
- Directories
- Contact forms
- Feedback forms

If you use these methods you will end up, at the very least, getting your company and website a bad name, as people hate spam and therefore hate the people who use it.

The other problem with using this software is that you have no real knowledge of sites your links could appear on and how you will be linked to them. The last thing you want is to have your link appearing in bad neighborhoods as this could seriously harm your website and even your company.

Beware

Spamming people's websites is a sure way to get your site a bad name.

Hot tip

Stay away from automated link-building software as it will rarely benefit your site.

Beware

Do not link out to websites that are spamming or you could be penalized.

Internal Linking

Internal links are those that you use within your own website to link your pages together, enabling searchers to navigate around your site.

There are two different types of internal link that you can use to navigate around your website:

Absolute links

Absolute links use the whole URL including the domain name and extension.

```
                                          <h2 class="swit
                                          <div class="hom
                                             <a href
a href="http://www.ineasysteps.com/books/details/?1840783184">
a href="./books/details/?1840783222"><img src="./images/books/
a href="./books/details/?1840782870"><img src="./images/books/
a href="./books/details/?1840783001"><img src="./images/books/
a href="./books/details/?9781840783247"><img src="./images/boo
```

Relative links

Relative links use addresses that are relative to where the link is placed on your website. They are the most commonly used.

```
a href="./books/details/?1840783184"><img src=".
a href="./books/details/?1840783222"><img src=".
a href="./books/details/?1840782870"><img src=".
a href="./books/details/?1840783001"><img src=".
```

During the design phase of a website, it is easy to overlook the detail of the links used to navigate around them, or more importantly, the text within those links. This is called anchor text and it contains the hyperlink that takes you to the other pages on the site.

Lost?
Our <u>site map</u> can help you find the page you need.

The text "site map" is the anchor text in this example and if clicked it will take you to the sitemap page.

You can really help add to the strength of your website theme by making use of the anchor text in your internal links.

Most internal links will have "click here" as the anchor text but this is pointless and adds no relevance to your website whatsoever. Instead of using "click here" as the anchor text you should be using the relevant keywords for that page, as this will add relevance and help Google to see what the page is about.

For example, if the page you are linking to is the one that you have optimized for the search phrase "Google Book", then make sure that the internal links you are using to link to that page make use of that keyword.

You do not always have to use the link text "Google Book"; remember you can use semantically similar words and words that will be relevant to that page, including:

- Google Books
- Book on Google
- Optimizing your website for Google
- Google SEO
- Getting your website found on Google
- SEO for Google

Beware

Ensure that you only use relevant keywords to link your pages together.

The other great thing about mixing your anchor text up is that it will not only look more natural but it will also stand a higher chance of ranking under a mixture of all of the keywords used.

Optimizing your link anchor text is easy to do and helps build relevance for your website and the pages that the links refer to.

By using optimized link anchor text instead of irrelevant text such as "click here" you will be:

- Optimizing your website for your keywords
- Helping your website visitors navigate easily
- Helping Google ascertain what your pages are about
- Strengthening your website theme

Finding Links

Most people struggle when finding places to get links from but it is actually relatively simple. Below are some common ways to find links:

Ask Google

One easy way to find links is to ask Google. To do this follow the steps below:

① Open up Google

② Carry out a search for your desired keywords

③ Navigate to the top sites to see whether they allow you to submit a link

Alternative option

① Open up Google

② Search for your niche (for us it would be "Google Book") and include "+links, +link, +site" at the end of your keywords. Google will look for sites that contain references to each

③ Then just submit your link to the relevant sites

Finding links in Linkdex

① Load Linkdex and select the Link Analysis tab

2 Select your competitor from the drop down list

You can select to see only the influential links by selecting this button

Domains & Links   FAQ

Select competitor to add   Select   ⟂   Only Show Influential ☐ Show Timelines ☐

Sites: Please select a domain

3 Now select the Site Types link from the Competitor Charts menu and you can review the spread of links defined by type

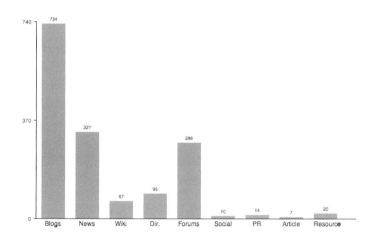

Hot tip

Reviewing a competitors link spread is very good for seeing what types of links are working for them

4 You can also review which keyword anchor text is being used and the most linked to pages by selecting the links from the Competitor Tables menu

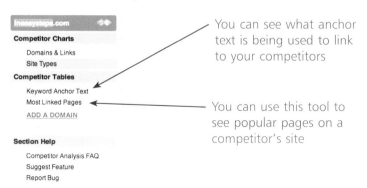

You can see what anchor text is being used to link to your competitors

You can use this tool to see popular pages on a competitor's site

How to Request Links

Once you have identified those sites you would like to get links from, you need to find a way of requesting them.

There are two ways of doing this depending on which method they would like you to adopt.

Don't forget

Spend some time on each of the forms so that your details read correctly, as badly filled-in forms will not be accepted.

The form

The first and most common option is a standard form on their website for you to fill in to request a link:

Enter a specific title relating to your product/service and remember to include your relevant keywords

Enter your URL

Here you can write a description of your product/service. You need to make sure you pick relevant keywords to add here as this will help increase your relevance for Google's natural listings

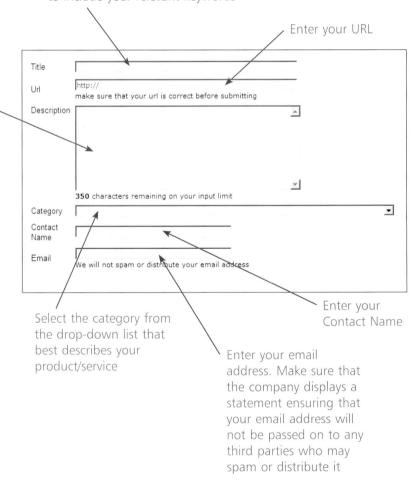

Select the category from the drop-down list that best describes your product/service

Enter your Contact Name

Enter your email address. Make sure that the company displays a statement ensuring that your email address will not be passed on to any third parties who may spam or distribute it

The email

Some site owners ask that you email them your request (or you will have seen that your site can add value to their visitors and discover that email is their preferred method of approach).

It is very important that when you send an email requesting a link for your website you take the time to construct it properly. If you do not spend time on the email to personalize it and get your message across, the likelihood is your email will go directly into their deleted items folder.

There is plenty of automated software out there that can just select a long list of websites and send the same generic email to them all. On the face of it this sounds tempting as it doesn't take very long but the actual links you will get out of it will be disappointingly few.

To really make the most of your linking you need to send a personal email to the owner of the site or the person named on it as the email contact, remembering the following:

- Try to use their name – it looks more personal and less automated

- Introduce yourself, your website and your company

- Compliment them on their website and say which bits you liked

- Tell them why they should link to your website

- Explain the benefits of linking to you for them and their visitors

- Tell them where you have placed their link, if applicable

- Suggest how they should link to your site, what page you would like your link to be on, what page to link to and the text to use

- Thank them for their time

- Sign it from yourself

Remember that when requesting links you need to be personal and properly explain why they should link to you to get the most out of the arrangement.

Hot tip

Personalized emails will get a more positive response.

119

Resource Page

If you are going to be linking to other people's websites the chances are you are going to need to reciprocate some of the links.

You will therefore need a page on which to place the links that you will reciprocate.

To set up this page you will need to create a new page using your website design package and name it appropriately.

For our "Google Book" website we would name our page something like:

Don't forget

You only want to accept relevant links into your resource page to help build your website theme.

- /google-book-resources

- /google-seo-resources

- /google-optimization-resources

- /google-book-links

- /google-seo-links

- /google-optimization-links

Once you have created this page you should put some text on it to describe the content. This should inform visitors that this is a page of resources that you feel they will find useful and relevant.

You should also include instructions on how people could add their links to this page. This could be a simple message explaining: "To appear here please link to our website using one of the following links". You will of course need to mention that their website should be relevant to your subject or it will not be included.

You would then create several different links that they could choose from, all with relevant and optimized anchor text to help your website gain relevance.

You can give your visitors two ways of submitting their links to you, by either:

- Using a form, or

- Emailing you their links

Let the Links Come to You

One of the most effective ways to get incoming links is by letting them come to you.

If you have created a strong website with good, unique and relevant content then people will naturally want to link to you to enhance the value to their visitors.

Attracting links in this way has now become known as link baiting and although it sounds dubious it is actually a logical and useful way of attracting links to your website. You can better equip your site to do this in several different ways:

- Offer something unique that can only be found on your website

- Give something away, such as a report or a document

- Have a unique online tool

- Coin a new saying or phrase in your industry and get people talking about it

- Give away a tool that others can use on their websites but only by linking back to you

- Have a game or quiz

- Be the first to document something

- Upload a useful film or documentary

- Become an expert in your niche and write about it

There are many different ways of doing this but you will need to find one that sits well within your website and industry.

Doing this will not only increase your inward links but you will find that:

- The links will come from sites to which you could not ordinarily submit a request

- The links will look more natural

- The anchor text will be varied, enabling your website to rank for more keywords

- Your website's relevance will increase

Hot tip

Link baiting will save you time as you will gain links naturally.

Links You Need

There are links you need and links you don't. Get the right links and this will help your website achieve higher positions in Google. Get the wrong links and your efforts will be wasted.

Links you need

- Are from well-known websites

- Are from sites with a high PageRank

- Are from sites with few links on the page

- Are from sites that have relevant, optimized anchor text

- Are from sites with a relevant theme

- Are static with a normal hyperlink

Links you do not need

- Are from non-relevant pages

- Are from unethical websites that use spam

- Are from pages with hundreds of non-related links

- Are hidden from the searchers' view

To see how important a website is to Google we can use the PageRank bar in the Google toolbar to help us decide.

Don't forget

You must only work to gain links from relevant websites.

122

You should look at the PageRank for not only the home page but also the page where your link would be placed. If it is full of links it will not be worth as much to you, as the PageRank will be split between all of the links on that page.

You should always try to get inward, rather than reciprocal links. They are far more valuable.

Get the Most From Your Links

To get the most from your links you need to make sure you do the following:

- Get links from pages with a good PageRank

- Make sure the sites are relevant to yours

- Vary the keywords that you use in the anchor text

- Vary the descriptions in your link

You must select the right place to put your links in order to get the most relevance from them, and ensure the website has a good PageRank:

Good PageRank

Great PageRank

Beware

Don't use the same anchor text all of the time; it will look unnatural to Google.

Hot tip

Try to get links from pages with relatively few on them. You'll get a greater share of the vote.

The higher the PageRank of the page, the more valuable a link on that site would be. You need to remember that the number of links on a page will influence how much of the vote you get; fewer links mean you will get more of the vote.

The main thing you must do is vary the keywords you use as your anchor text. This is important as it will look more natural, and because it looks more natural you will most likely achieve higher positions. Google knows which words are similar and by using similar keywords you will be optimizing for all of them at the same time.

Directory Linking

Directory linking is a great way to source links for your website.

A directory is simply a website that houses links to other sites and places them in an organized order. This makes it easier for people to find what they are looking for. There are thousands out there, from general directories to specialist niche listings.

Some directories are free but with others, like the Yahoo directory, you have to pay to be included. This being said, most of the directories charge only a few dollars to submit your link.

You can use directories to gain many useful links from relevant categories and in most of them you can even choose your own anchor text and descriptions.

To find directories relevant to your industry, you can simply ask Google again.

To do this follow the steps below:

1. Navigate to the Google search box. Following on with the keyword that we have been using as an example, you would type "directory+google book" into the search box and click Search

This will then return a list of directories which could provide useful links.

Hot tip

Directory linking will help you to increase your inward links drastically.

There is also a handy list that has been created, with many of the directories in it and information on each of them.

The directory list is also split into sections for different industries to make it easier to navigate, and it can be downloaded as a free Excel spreadsheet.

Don't forget

Spend the time to submit to the directories properly otherwise they will just delete your application, as they do not have time to fill in the gaps.

①　Navigate to http://info.vilesilencer.com/top

②　Click the Excel Download link

③　Click Save to save the list to your computer so that you can refer back to it at a later date

The great benefit with directory linking is that most of them do not require a reciprocal link, so this is an easy way of building quality, inward non-reciprocal links to your website.

Furthermore, because directories take varying amounts of time to assess and add your link to their listings, you will be on the receiving end of a steady, gradual stream of new links which will look more natural to the search engines.

Effective Articles

Writing articles is also a very good way to gain inward links into your website. The way to do this is by writing articles on your niche subject. This will help you not only to generate a good number of inward links to your website but to establish yourself as an authority in your field.

Writing your articles

Beware

If you write your article as sales copy, people will tend not to use it.

When you write an article it can be on any subject as long as it will be relevant to your website. After all, if it is not relevant you will struggle to get it on the websites that will give you the best links. It is important to remember when writing your article to:

- Make it relevant to your niche

- Keep on track and structure it well

- Ensure that the article will benefit your readers

- Avoid promoting your own website or business in the text

Getting your articles noticed

Once you have written your article you will need to distribute it and you can do this in several different ways:

- Submit your article to related niche websites

- Use article submission software

You can seek out and submit your article to niche websites that specialize in your area of expertise. To do this just follow these instructions:

1. In the Google search box type article+keyword. So, using our previous example, we have typed "article+google book"

2. See if the sites you find will accept your article

The second option is the easiest way to distribute your articles, and that is to use article submission software. One submission service is available at www.goarticles.com:

1 Navigate to www.goarticles.com

Hot tip

Ezine Articles is another great place to submit your articles and can be found by navigating to www.ezinearticles.com.

2 Click the link to Register

3 Fill out the Personal Information form and click Process Application

GoArticles Member Registration Form

All fields are required

Name:	
Email Address:	
City:	
State/Province:	
Country:	Select Country
Password:	
Password (again):	

☐ I have read the Terms of Service & Privacy Statement and agree that GoArticles may send me email notices.

[Add Me...]

Hot tip

Using article submission software will get your article distributed more easily and save you time.

4 You will now be able to submit your articles

Buying Links

To secure that top position on Google, more and more emphasis is now being placed on a website's link popularity. So surely, a quick and easy option would be to simply buy some...

Unfortunately, Google frowns upon this and views it as PageRank manipulation. As such, it will punish any websites it finds taking part in either the buying or selling of links.

Google does state that "buying and selling links is a normal part of the economy of the web when done for advertising purposes, and not for the manipulation of search results".

If you do buy links for "advertising purposes" Google states that you must either:

Beware

If Google believes you are buying or selling links to bias PageRank they will penalize your website.

- Add a rel="nofollow" attribute to the <a> tag

- Redirect the links to an intermediate page that is blocked from the search engines with a robots.txt file

This would then allow you to have the link but would not allow any credibility or PageRank to be passed to your website, ensuring that the link is not bought for the purpose of manipulating PageRank.

There are many websites out there that seem to be involved in the buying and selling of links and seem to be doing very well from it.

Text Link Ads is one of those websites that allows people to buy and sell links.

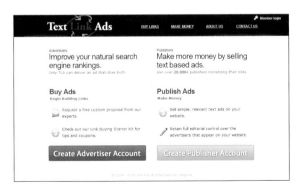

I would always recommend avoiding the buying and selling of links as the cost of getting caught is prohibitive and there are other more ethical ways of securing top quality links.

Online PR

Press releases are a great way to get your business both increased exposure online and to generate good one-way links.

Many of the top press release submission sites will also have an option for submitting your press releases to places like Google News.

These sites are monitored by journalists working for the top news agencies like CNN and the BBC. Imagine the type of links possible if your press release was successfully picked up?

Writing your press release

When writing a press release it is important to remember to:

- Include a punchy title

- Include contact details in case further information is required

- Ensure your keywords are included

- Keep on track and structured

- Ensure it is newsworthy and if possible tie it in to something current

- Ensure it is free of typos and errors

Getting your press release noticed

There are many places you can submit your press releases to, ranging from free sites to those charging over $500 per submission.

PR Web is a paid-for resource but in my experience I have found no better resource for getting your press release exposed online; you will also be fed back valuable data on the number of times it has been picked up.

Forums

Forums provide a wealth of information. You can find answers to your questions and learn more about specific topics.

They can also be a valuable source of promotion for your website and generator of inward links.

When navigating your way around most forums, you will notice that at the bottom of each person's snippet, there is a signature.

You can put who you are within these signature blocks, and add in a link to your website.

Many people will just put their website address and nothing else, but to really get the best from these links you need to ensure that you use keyword-rich anchor text.

Ways to get the most out of forums

Beware

Do not attempt to spam forums or you will get banned and you may damage your reputation online.

- Ensure you include a keyword-rich link to your website in your email signature

- Join only a few specific forums

- Do not spam

- Be helpful and not always self promoting

How to find the best forum for your niche

To find out which forums you should contribute to, follow the process below:

1. In the Google search box type keyword+forum. Using our previous example we typed "book+forum"

2. Pick out the ones that seem most specific to your niche

3. Review the forum guidelines to ensure you will get a followed link that you can customize

10 Monitoring Your Results

It is essential to monitor your website optimization results so that you know what is working and what needs more attention. This involves keeping your website up to date and current so that Google will crawl it more regularly.

Checking Your Web Statistics

Every website should have its own site statistics package running as a standard feature.

This will feed back basic yet invaluable information about your website's performance and your visitors. This will help you to determine what is working and what you need to alter in order to increase your website's traffic. It will include such information as:

- Number of website visits

- Visit duration

- Countries your visitors are coming from

- When the search engines visit your website

- Most popular pages

- Entry pages

- Exit pages

- Time spent on pages

- Which operating system your visitors are using

- Which browser they are using

- Which keywords your visitors used to find you

- Which websites are sending visitors

- Links your website has gained and where they come from

- Any lost queries or problems with dead links

To access your website statistics, find out the URL that you need to enter and any login procedure required to access it.

You should have received this information from your website host. If you had your website built for you by a company then you should contact them to get it.

Don't forget

Web statistics show a true picture of how effective your optimization has been.

Your statistics will look something like this:

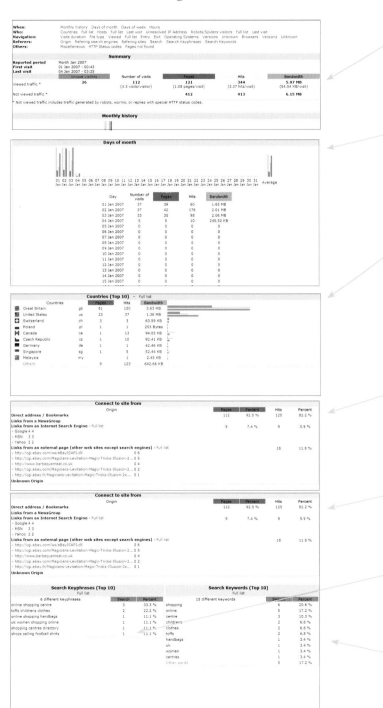

This includes a summary of your website's monthly visits

This gives a breakdown of your website's visits month on month

This breaks down your website's daily visits

This allows you to analyze your visits according to location

View the pages and links that connect to your website

View search phrases used in the search engines that lead to your website

View individual keywords used in searches that lead to your website

Using Google Analytics

Using your web statistics to tell you about your visitors is a good idea. Using Google Analytics to tell you everything you could possibly want to know about your visitors and your website is a great idea.

Google Analytics can tell you nearly everything about your website. The main features we will use are the Overview pages, and they are as follows:

- My dashboard
- Conversion goals overview
- Traffic sources overview
- Content overview
- In-Page analytics

My Dashboard

You can navigate to your dashboard by clicking the "Home" link. This can be customized to include popular features that include:

- Site visits and page views
- Time on site by country
- Daily visits
- Traffic types

Conversion goals overview

The conversion goals overview can be found by navigating to "Goals Overview" from the "Conversions Tab" and includes:

- How many goal completions you have had

- The ratio of conversions to visits

Hot tip

Keep a close eye on your top keywords as they can end up being different from those you would expect.

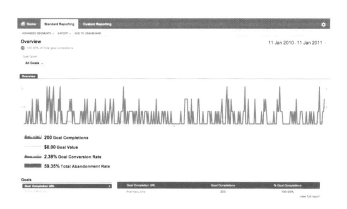

Traffic sources overview

The traffic sources overview can be found by navigating to "Overview" from the "Traffic Sources" tab and includes:

- Referral sources

- Keywords

- Landing page

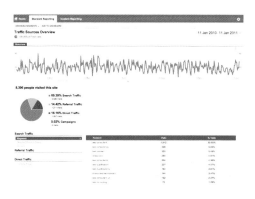

...cont'd

Content overview

The content overview can be found by navigating to "Overview" from the "Content" tab and includes:

- Entrance pages

- Exit pages

- Content pages

Hot tip

Keep an eye on the top exit pages – maybe you need to look at updating them to keep visitors interested.

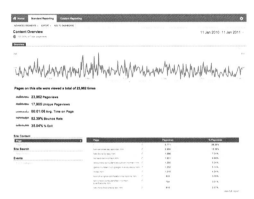

In-Page analytics

This will highlight the most popular pages and will provide you with a better understanding of how visitors navigate through your website. It can be found under the "Content" tab.

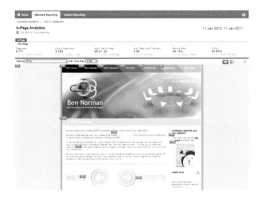

We have only covered the basic functions of Google Analytics here; there are many other features available.

Running Ranking Reports

Running ranking reports will feedback valuable information to you regarding where your website is currently ranked in Google's natural listings.

Running a ranking report will also help you to identify the following information:

- The keywords for which you have successfully optimized your website

- The keywords for which you need to do more optimization work

- Which keywords are responsible for the traffic you are receiving

5 steps to ensure you get the most from your website's ranking report

1. Make sure your list of desired keywords is up-to-date and in priority order

2. Ensure you track all priority keywords but don't try to track everything as you will lose focus on the main ones

3. Monitor your report at least once a month to ensure you are not missing important drops or gains in your website rankings

4. Add new keywords as you find them

5. Ensure that you also focus on long tail keywords

A ranking report will identify valuable information in the keywords you are targeting and the success you are achieving.

If you don't keep your keyword list up-to-date you will not get the most out of this very useful part of the analysis process and will defeat the point of doing it.

Hot tip

Look at your Google Analytics account to identify converting keywords that you're not tracking.

Don't forget

Run your reports regularly to monitor your search engine positions.

...cont'd

Use Linkdex

Using Linkdex to manage and run your ranking reports is particulary useful as you can then cross reference to see how well the pages are optimized for those words without leaving the tool.

To setup and run your ranking reports follow the below steps:

1 Open Linkdex and navigate to the "Rank Tracking" tab

2 To add your desired keywords, scroll down to the "Action" section and select either "Add Single Keywords" or "Bulk Upload Keywords"

Add Single Keywords

3 To add your keywords one by one, scroll down to the "Action" section and select "Add Single Keywords"

4 Add the keyword you would like to track

Add a keyword for rank tracking

Keyword
Expected page   /
Save   Cancel

5 Add the page you expect to rank for the term, if you think it will be the home page then just leave this section blank and click "Save"

138

Bulk Upload Keywords

1 To upload multiple keywords, scroll down to the "Action" section and select "Bulk Upload Keywords"

2 Select the .txt file with your desired keywords, ensuring each keyword is on a new line

Keywords Upload

Bulk Keyword Upload   Close   Never Show Again

This feature allows you to upload lots of keywords quickly and easily. Just follow these 4 easy steps:

- In an application like Excel create CSV file with your keywords in one column and optionally the URL of the page you think should rank for that keyword in the second column
- Now from the Bulk Upload page in Linkdex click "browse" and find the txt or csv file containing your keywords on your computer's hard drive and click 'upload'
- Check the information we found on the file you uploaded, editing where necessary
- When happy, click 'Save and Start Tracking Rankings', and Linkdex will begin tracking your rankings on these keywords and optimizing your websites pages

Upload a csv or txt file of keywords and optionally the pages you should rank for, with one keyword and page per line (File size limit is 1 MB).
You have credits available for 1 keywords at the normal checking rate.

[Choose File] No file chosen

[Upload] [Cancel]

3 Click the "Upload" button

4 Your new keywords will be added to the Rank Tracking system and will say "Not yet checked" until Linkdex updates them over the following 24 hours

	Keyword	Rank (UK)	Change	Page Ranked	Visits	Estimated Google Searches	Updated		
☐	computer book publisher Add Tag	...			configure		Not yet checked	✕	✎
☐	computer books Add Tag	11	/		configure	590	14 Jan	✕	✎
☐	in easy steps Add Tag	...			configure	140	Not yet checked	✕	✎
☐	in easy steps books Add Tag	...			configure		Not yet checked	✕	✎

...cont'd

Free Online Ranking Report

Another way to check your ranking results is to use a free online search engine ranking checker.

There are many of these around and a good one is available at www.mikes-marketing-tools.com/ranking-reports/ and is free to use at the time of printing.

Don't forget

Positions will move around from time to time.

1   Navigate to www.mikes-marketing-tools.com/ranking-reports/

2   Navigate to the Search Term box at the bottom of the page

3   Enter the URL and the search terms you would like to review, along with the search engines you would like to check them in and run the report

Don't forget

You may see different results in your ranking report to your browser if you are querying different data centers.

SEARCH	GOOGLE	YAHOO!	BING	AOL
'in easy steps books publisher' ineasysteps.com	1	1	2	1
'in easy steps books' ineasysteps.com (01/16/2012 - 05:06 PST)	1	1	1	1
'in easy steps' ineasysteps.com (01/16/2012 - 05:01 PST)	1	1	1	1

4   You can include as many search terms as you wish, with each one listed in a new window with their respective position in all applicable search engines

Analyzing Ranking Reports

Once you have created your ranking report you need to analyze the data to see the results of any changes you have made.

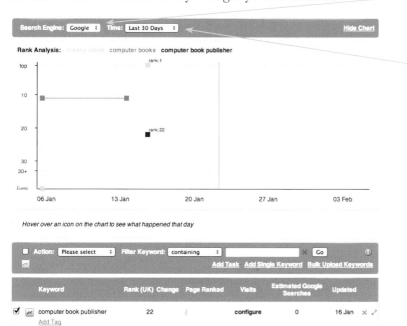

Select which search engine you wish to check

Select time frame

Hover over an icon on the chart to see what happened that day

Select the graph button to add the data to the graph

When you look at the report generated, you will be able to see and arrange your data in many different ways to enable you to get the most from it.

Your ranking report will tell you many things at a glance including:

- Pages added

- Pages removed

- Rank change

- Estimated Google searches

- Date updated

When analyzing your data, always bear in mind any changes you have made to your website so that you know what has been successful.

Site Analysis

When your positions change for the worse it is a sign that your website is out of date and is losing the relevance battle with Google.

To combat this and establish what needs to be done to regain your lost places, it is advisable to run regular analysis on your website's pages.

You should be running analysis on your site at least once per month but it is preferable to do this weekly.

Beware

Run regular analysis reports on your website to ensure you are keeping up to date with Google's algorithm.

Optimization	Score	Analysis	Action
Body Text More details	☺	There are 151 words contained in the body content. This is under the 300 word recommended minimum. Could you add more unique useful content on this topic for readers?	Add Task
Duplicate Content More details	Choose Score ⁞	Use Google Webmaster Tools to check that this page is considered unique by Google.	Add Task
Meta Appeal More details	Choose Score ⁞	If your page title and description were ranked at #3 would you click on your business first?	Add Task
Meta Page Description More details	☺	You have specified you page description but it's over 160 characters. Shortening it will ensure all of your description gets read.	Add Task
URL Status More details	☑	This page is being redirected using a 301 redirect, and tells Google that this page has permanently moved to a new location. Read what Google has to say about redirects.	Add Task
Page Links More details	Choose Score ⁞	Use Google Webmaster Tools to review the internal and external links pointing at this page.	Add Task
Title tag Format and Length More details	☑	Good news. Your page title is more than 40 characters and less than the 65 character recommended limit.	Add Task
W3C Validity More details	Choose Score ⁞	Use the W3C code validity tool to check if this page has code issues.	Add Task
Headings (H1,H2,H3) More details	⚠	You have not used your keyword/phrase in any heading on this page.	Add Task

Re-run your site analysis report

1 Open Linkdex and then select "Site Optimization" from main menu

2 Select which page you would like to analyse

3 Review the overall score and make sure it hasn't dropped

4 Work through the recommended changes and re-optimize the relevant sections

Link Analysis

As you have seen previously, links play an important part in the optimization process and you should pay close attention to how many links you have secured.

There are two ways in which to check this with ease:

Ask Google

Navigate to your home page and use the Google toolbar to tell you who points to your website:

Hot tip

You can also check your backward links from the SEO Site Tools plug in if you are using Google Chrome.

1   Navigate to your website

2   Right-click on this page and select the Backward Links option from the Page info category

3   Google will now display a list of your current inward links

In Easy Steps: Web Graphics in easy steps
About the author. Mary Lojkine has been writing about computers and technology for more than a decade. Her areas of expertise include the Internet, ...
www.ineasysteps.com/books/details/?1840782315 - 16k - Cached - Similar pages

In Easy Steps: Tell a friend
Tell a friend. Fill in this form and submit it to your friend. You can edit the message text if you wish. Your friend will then receive the information as ...
www.ineasysteps.com/site/tell/?1840782714 - 15k - Cached - Similar pages

4   You should now compare these with your previous list of inward links to see which links you have gained now

...cont'd

Use Linkdex

This is particularly useful as it allows you to see why you are doing well with certain keywords.

① Open Linkdex and click the Link Analysis tab

② Select your site from the drop-down list and you will see the total links to your website and also total domains that link to it

Domains & Links   FAQ

Select competitor to add [Select   ⁝]   Only Show Influential ☐ Show Timelines ☐
Sites: Please select a domain

③ Select the "Show Timelines" feature to visibly demonstrate the growth of your link profile and to see the dates links were added

06 Jan

[play]   [reset]

④ Select the "Site Types" option to see where your links are coming from as this will tell you what is helping you rank and if you are missing certain types of links

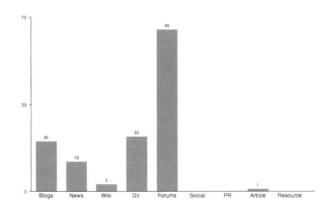

5 Select "Keyword Anchor Text" from the "Competitor Tables" menu which will show you the most popular anchor text that is being used to link to your website

Anchor Text Frequency

Select competitor to add | Select ⬦

Sites: ineasysteps.com ✕

Anchor Text	Count
www.ineasysteps.com	71
In Easy Steps	56
http://www.ineasysteps.com/	48
http://www.ineasysteps.com/resources/articles/read/?id=10	30
"Understanding Camera Raw"	30
Computer Step	25
In Easy Steps Limited	22

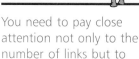

Don't forget

You need to pay close attention not only to the number of links but to the anchor text used.

6 Select "Most Linked Pages" from the "Competitor Tables" menu and this will show you the pages of your website that people are linking to the most

Linked Pages

Select competitor to add | Select ⬦

Sites: ineasysteps.com ✕

Page	Count
http://www.ineasysteps.com/	149
http://www.ineasysteps.com	142
http://www.ineasysteps.com/resources/articles/read/?id=10	34
http://www.ineasysteps.com/books/details/?1840783036	19
http://www.ineasysteps.com/books/details/?184078282x	18
http://www.ineasysteps.com/books/details/?1840782951	17
http://www.ineasysteps.com/books/explore/programming/	15
http://www.ineasysteps.com/books/?1840782757	13
http://www.ineasysteps.com/books/?1840782072	11

7 Once you have analysed your links you can keep coming back and repeating the process, using the timeline to see the new links that have been added

...cont'd

Use SEO Site Tools

SEO Site Tools is extremely useful when looking to carry out a quick check on your link profile.

As well as using it to review your own link profile, you can also use SEO Site Tools to spy on your competitors.

1. Navigate to your website and select the SEO Site Tools icon

ajdbpjdeomopbpkjjc

2. You can now analyse your link profile through the "External Page Data" section

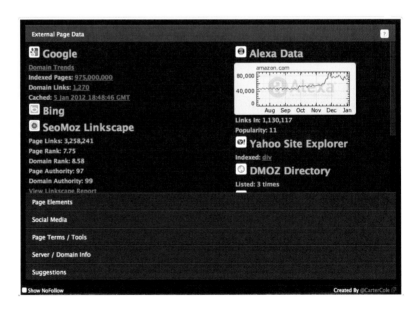

3. You should keep a record of the figures produced by this report and you can then compare this over time to both your website and also your competitors

Competition Analysis

In order to get to and remain at the top of the search results for your desired search terms, it is essential that you keep an eye on your competition.

To maintain or improve your rankings, it is essential that you compete with the sites around you and ensure that your pages are stronger and more relevant at all times

Monitoring your competition lets you know:

- What they are doing to their websites
- If their positions have changed
- What they are doing right
- What they are doing wrong

This will aid you in optimizing your website further and keeping one step ahead of your competition.

In order to analyze your competition effectively, you should compare their progress with that of your own site.

To analyze and compare your website to your competitor's website follow the instructions starting on p51.

Hot tip

Analyzing your competition will ensure that you always know what they are doing and how.

147

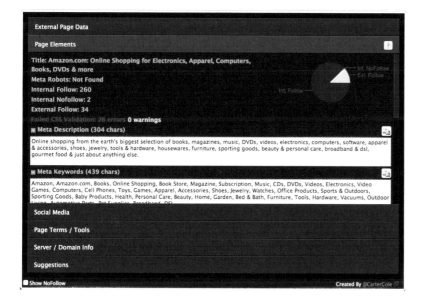

Keeping Up To Date

You will undoubtedly be making regular adjustments to your website and adding new content to keep it current.

When updating your site, it is important to ensure that your existing content and links are reviewed.

For instance, when a new page is added or an old one removed, this should be reflected in the sitemap as well as in all other internal links that are affected.

Potential problems

- Causing errors when your sitemap is crawled
- Giving Google incorrect information
- Creating inconsistencies in your website's structure

What to update

- Update the website sitemap
- Update the Google sitemap
- Update the website navigation
- Install the Google Analytics code for the page
- Update your Google AdWords campaign (see p154)
- Update keywords in the ranking checker tool

Google can tell how often your website is updated. If you keep it fresh and current, the spiders will crawl it more frequently.

Google prefers websites that are regularly updated as the content they display is much more likely to be relevant when compared to less frequently changed sites.

This can be beneficial as you will not have to wait as long to see the effects of your optimization efforts.

This will help Google to identify the theme of your site and view it as a source of useful, relevant information on a particular subject

Hot tip

If Google sees that your website is updated frequently it will begin to check it more regularly.

Adding New Pages

If you are to have a successful and relevant website you should be adding new content regularly.

To remain relevant and to develop your rankings, you need to continually develop new content.

When adding new content ensure

- You know what keywords you are targeting with it

- You add the new keywords to your ranking tool so that it will monitor their positions

- You put them in the appropriate place

- You have updated your sitemap and the Google sitemap

- You have used appropriate anchor text for the internal links to the page

The most important thing to do when adding new content is to make sure you know which keywords you are targeting with the new pages.

This will ensure that your content stays focused and includes your desired keywords. If your content does not include your keywords then it will not be very easy for Google to find its relevance.

When adding the new pages ensure

- Your keywords are used in the content

- You are also using semantically similar words

- You have related keywords in the internal links that point to the page

- Your keywords are in the Alt tags

- Your keywords are in the Meta and Title tags

Following these simple guidelines will assist Google hugely when it comes to assessing the relevance of your content.

As a result, it should also help you to achieve strong rankings for your pages.

Hot tip

Ensure your page name makes use of the main keywords for the page.

Beware

If you do not use your keywords in your new pages you will stand little chance of ranking well for them.

Don't forget

See Chapter 6 for more information on adding new pages.

Removing Content

At some point in time you will need to remove a page on your website.

This is an easy enough operation in itself, but you must ensure that you update the site to reflect the fact that the page is no longer present.

If you fail to do so your visitors could end up landing on a page like the one shown below, and navigating away from your website:

In Easy Steps Error 404
(File does not exist)

The URL that you requested, /wrong page, could not be found. Perhaps you either mistyped the URL or we have a broken link.

We have logged this error and will correct the problem if it is a broken link.

Please Click Here to Return to our Home Page.

What to do before removing content

- Remove all links and references to the page

- Update your website's sitemap

- Update your Google sitemap

- Set up a 301 redirect to the new or most relevant page

What to check after you remove the page from your website

- Make sure your redirect is working by entering the URL for the old page and ensuring you are redirected to the new page

- If anyone was linking to the old page, contact them and ask them to update their link

When emailing people who had linked to the old page, ask them to amend the link to go to a new page on your website to ensure that the PageRank is passed on.

Supplemental Index

So that Google can keep its index as efficient as possible it has two different indexes: its main index and its supplemental index.

Web pages in Google's supplemental index are not deemed as important as the pages stored in its main index and as such will not receive as much of their resources. This means that those pages are less likely to be crawled as often as the pages in its main index.

There are many reasons your web pages could be put into the supplemental index e.g. if it is very similar to another page, the page size is too big or the page is causing issues when crawled.

Pages in the supplemental index will have significantly less chance of being returned to a searcher than those in the main index.

To make sure your web pages do not end up in Google's supplemental index ensure that all of them:

- Contain unique and useful content
- Have deep links coming into them (p112)
- Have unique Meta, and titles
- Validate so they don't have problems being crawled

To work out how many pages of your website are in Google's supplemental index you need to look at the following:

Total pages indexed:

site:www.yourwebsite.com

Pages in Google's main index:

site:www.yourwebsite.com -inallurl:www.yourwebsite.com

To work out the number of pages in Google's supplemental index you just subtract the number of pages in Google's main index from the total pages indexed. You will then have the number of pages from your website that are in Google's supplemental index.

Google Display Variations

When it comes to Google's results page, more is most definitely more and the more space you can take up the more chance you have of visitors clicking on your ad.

As well as the standard ad, there are two further ads on the organic side. If you can show real relevance, you may be awarded them. These include:

Sitelinks ad

SEO Consultant / SEO Services
www.ben-norman.co.uk/
Professional SEO Services from Google SEO Consultant **Ben Norman**, a UK based SEO Consultant and Published Author on the subject specialising in Organic ...
Contact Me - SEO Services - Ben Norman - Get to #1 on Google In Easy Steps
You shared this

The sitelinks ad is structured as above where other relevant pages from the website are then listed underneath in a row.

The sitelinks ad is great for drawing attention to your website. Visitors are also more likely to click on it.

Expanded sitelinks ad

www.koozai.com/
Award Winning Digital Marketing Agency. Search Engine Optimisation (SEO) and Pay per Click (PPC) Specialists. FREE Analysis Report; No Obligation Quote.
You shared this

Digital Marketing Blog
Koozai's Digital Marketing Blog Offering the Latest News, Help ...

About Us
Award-Winning London and Southampton SEO Agency ...

Search Engine Marketing
Koozai Are a Search Engine Marketing (SEM) Company ...

Case Studies
View Online Marketing Case Studies from the Clients of UK ...

Contact Us
Contact Digital Agency **Koozai** to Discuss Our Award-Winning ...

Meet The Team
Leading Marketing Agency Koozai Employ a Team of Professional ...

More results from koozai.com »

When more than one website page has relevance for a given search phrase, the extended sitelinks ad is given.

The relevant links would then appear in the extended part of the sitelinks ad, enabling easy navigation for the searcher to find the most relevant page within the website for their query.

11 Google AdWords

Google AdWords is your key to instant online visibility. You can pick specific keywords to target and have your website appearing for them in under an hour. It is important that your account is set up properly to ensure you get the desired results.

What is Google AdWords?

Google AdWords is a pay-per-click program run by Google.

What this means is that instead of earning positions as in the natural listings, you can pay to be seen.

Google divides its search engine real estate into two parts:

- Natural listings
- Sponsored listings

Natural listings as you know cannot be bought, only earned through relevance, so good positions are only achievable through optimizing your website.

By using Google AdWords you will appear in the sponsored listings (that are displayed above and alongside the natural listings) by agreeing to pay if someone clicks on your ads.

At first this sounds very expensive but, if managed correctly, the costs involved are very reasonable considering the visibility and targeted traffic you will receive.

You will only have to pay a fee when you receive clicks on your ad. This means that you will only pay when Google sends someone to your website. The price of your clicks will vary depending on the industry you are in and the competition bidding on your specific keywords.

Don't forget

Google AdWords will only be cost-effective if set up and managed correctly.

Sponsored listings

Natural listings

What are the Benefits?

Google AdWords is a very important tool in your online marketing arsenal.

The reason this is such an important tool is that you can be on the first page of Google within just minutes of opening your AdWords account. Not only this, but you can actually choose the keywords for which you wish to appear.

With AdWords you can create your ad and choose your keywords, save them and then be seen on Google in an instant. This is unlike optimizing your website, where you have to wait for the search engines to update and continually optimize for better results.

Google AdWords benefits

- Reach out to over 80% of internet users

- Target specific countries or areas

- Gain an instant Google position

- Choose your own keywords

- Create your own ad

- Split test ads to increase efficiency

- Decide which page to take the searchers to

- Track conversions

- Make instant changes to increase conversions

- Select a daily budget

The main benefit of using AdWords is that you can instantly appear under your desired keywords and have your website seen by people who are interested in what you are offering.

This makes the sales process easier as you do not have to convince people to buy what you are selling – they are already looking for it.

This ensures that your conversion rates will be higher than if you target people at random with other forms of advertising.

Don't forget

Google not only displays ads on Google – they appear on its partner sites too.

Beware

If your ads are not set up to be relevant, your campaign will not be financially efficient.

Setting up Your Account

To set up your Google AdWords account just follow the simple steps below:

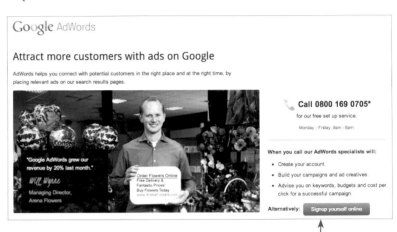

1 Navigate to Google AdWords and click the "Signup yourself online" button

2 Select the following options and then sign in with your existing login information

You can use this option as you already have a Google account

It is easier to use the same account

Login to your existing account

Create Google Account   Set time zone and currency   Verify account

Create Google Account

Hello, and welcome to Google AdWords. We're glad to have you on board! We need just a few details from you in order to set up your account.

To begin creating your AdWords account, choose the username and password that you'd like to use with AdWords.

Which best describes you?
- I have an email address and password that I already use with Google services like AdSense, Google Mail, Orkut or iGoogle.
- I do *not* use these other services.

Would you like to have a single account for all Google services?
You can use your existing Google account email address and password for AdWords as well. Or you can choose new ones just for AdWords.
- I'd like to use my existing Google account for AdWords.
- I'd like to choose a new login name and password just for AdWords.

Sign in to AdWords with the *existing* email address and password that you use to access other Google services.

Google **Account**

Email: _____
e.g. pat@example.com
Password: _____
☑ Stay signed in
[Sign in]

Can't access your account?

Select your time zone and currency preferences and click continue

✓ Create Google Account   Set time zone and currency   Verify account

Set your time zone and currency preferences

We need two more details to set up your AdWords account: the currency that you'll use to pay Google for your advertising costs, and the time zone that you'd like your reports to be in.
You won't be able to change these details later, so please be careful when making your selections.

Select a permanent time zone for your account.
This will be the time zone for all your account reporting and billing.

Time zone country or territory: | United States ▼ |

Time zone: | (GMT-06:00) Central Time ▼ |

Select a permanent currency for your account.
Review the available payment options for local currencies before you decide. Not all currencies are available in all areas.

| US Dollar (USD $) ▼ |

Your time zone and currency settings can't be changed after you set up your account.
Please review your choices carefully and then click 'Continue'.

[Back] [Continue]

 Your AdWords account has now been created

✓ Create Google Account   ✓ Set time zone and currency   ✓ Verify account

Your AdWords account has been created

Next step: Create your first ad campaign.

Login Email:

You can now sign in to your AdWords account using the Google Account address and password you just specified. When you sign in, you'll be asked to create your first ad campaign and enter your billing information to activate your account and start running your ads. We'll also send an activation email with more details to the address listed above.

Your ad won't run until you submit your billing information.

Sign in to your AdWords account

Start learning how to make the most of your AdWords account by reading our optimisation tips.

 Now sign in to your account and you can create your first Google AdWords campaign

Creating Your First Campaign

The secret of a successful AdWords campaign lies not only in the selection of relevent keywords and effective ad copy but in the campaign settings themselves.

1 Navigate to Google AdWords and sign in, you can now create your first campaign

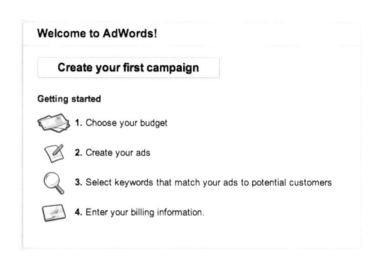

2 Select your campaign type, I would suggest selecting "Search Network only" as this will allow for better targeting on Google

3 Name your campaign something specific so you can easily find it when you have several campaigns running

4 Select the location(s) you would like to target and the languages your customers speak

Locations and languages

Locations ?	In what geographical locations do you want your ads to be displayed?	
	◯ All countries and territories	
	● United Kingdom	
	◯ Let me choose...	
	Enter a location such as a city, region or country	Show map
Languages ?	What languages do you customers speak?	
	English Edit	
☐ Advanced location options		
Targeting method ?	● Target using either physical location or search intent (recommended) ?	
Search Network only	◯ Target using physical location: Device-based location signals ?	
	◯ Target using search intent: Location terms in user queries ?	

I would recommend leaving the advanced location options as standard

5 Select the networks and devices you wish your ads to show on, I recommend switching off the display network and mobile devices and tablets to conserve your budget

Networks and devices

Networks ?	◯ All available sites (Recommended for new advertisers)
	● Let me choose...
	Search ☑ Google Search
	☑ Search partners (requires Google search)
	Display ☐ Display Network ?
	• Broad reach: Show ads on pages that match my primary targeting method ?
	Example: Show ads if keywords match
	Specific reach: Show ads only on pages that match all my targeting methods ?
	Example: Show ads only if both keywords and placements match
	♀ Your ads won't be displayed on Google's Display Network. Learn more
Devices ?	◯ All available devices (Recommended for new advertisers)
	● Let me choose...
	☑ Desktop and laptop computers
	☐ Mobile devices with full browsers
	☐ Tablets with full browsers
	? Advanced mobile and tablet options
	♀ Your ads won't show on mobile devices.
	Your ads won't show on tablets.

6 Set your default bid and daily budget, this will apply to the first ad group in the campaign

Bidding and budget

Bidding option ?	Basic options | Advanced options
	◯ I'll manually set my bids for clicks
	● AdWords will set my bids to help maximise clicks within my target budget
Budget ?	$ [ ] per day
	Actual daily spend may vary ?
☐ Delivery method (advanced)	
Delivery method ?	**Standard: Display ads evenly over time**
	Accelerated delivery is unavailable for the selected bidding option.

7 I would recommend that you take the tour to review what the below options will do so you can review if your campaign will benefit from them

Ad extensions

You can use this optional feature to include relevant business information with your ads. Take a tour.

Location	?	☐ Extend my ads with location information
Sitelinks	?	☐ Extend my ads with links to sections on my site
Call	?	☐ Extend my ads with a phone number
Social	?	☐ Increase the social relevance of my ads by associating them with my Google+ Page

8 If you would prefer for your ads not to run 24/7 you should use the below ad scheduling settings

Advanced settings

☐ Schedule: Start date, end date, ad scheduling

Start date   `12 Jan 2012`

End date   ⦿ None
              ◯ `_____`

Ad scheduling ? **Display ads all days and hours**

Automatic bidding campaigns may not use ad scheduling ?

9 You should select the "Rotate: Show ads more evenly" option as we will need this later when we cover ad split testing

☐ Ad delivery: Ad rotation, frequency capping

Ad rotation ? ⦿ Optimise for clicks: Show ads expected to provide more clicks
                  Optimise for conversions: Show ads expected to provide more conversions
                  Unavailable because conversion tracking isn't set up. Setup conversion tracking.
                  ◯ Rotate: Show ads more evenly

Frequency capping ? ⦿ No cap on impressions
Display Network only ◯ `_____` Impressions per day ▾ per ad group ▾

10 We will not be using the below options so you can click "Save and continue" to finish creating your first campaign

☐ Demographic bidding
Demographic ? Set bidding preferences for specific demographics on eligible content network sites.
Display Network only Edit

☐ Social settings
+1 on Display Network ? ⦿ Include the +1 button and the +1 annotations on my ads on the Display Network.
Display Network only ◯ Do not include the +1 button and the +1 annotations on my ads on the Display Network.

☐ Automatic campaign optimisation (Display Network only)
Targeting mode ? **Standard: Show ads based on targeting elements such as keywords and placements.**
Auto-optimised targeting mode is not available because conversion tracking isn't set up. Set up conversion tracking.

Save and continue   Cancel new campaign

Writing the Perfect Ad

The secret of a successful AdWords campaign lies not only in the selection of keywords but also in the creation of an effective advert.

People will often consider a number of factors before clicking on an advert. Relevance is usually top of this list, which is why you need to be able to convey your message succinctly within the ad text.

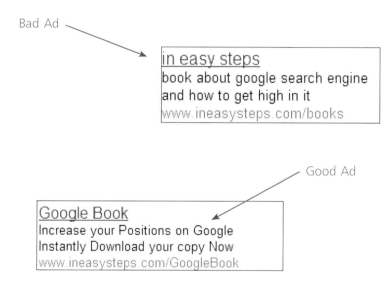

Remember you need to create individual ad groups for each of your products or services. This will enable you to target specific areas, which will increase the relevance of each of your ads.

This in turn will increase your conversion rates and the efficiency of your campaign. Do not be tempted to create just one ad for all of your keywords as it will not be as efficient or cost-effective.

Ensure your ad:

- Does not use your company name in the title
- Includes your keywords
- Mentions a benefit
- Capitalizes on important words

URLs

Your URL is also an important part of your ad and can be used to add relevance.

With the URL part of your ad you can select both the URL text that is seen and the page the searcher is taken to.

Your destination URL and the display URL are not and should not be the same.

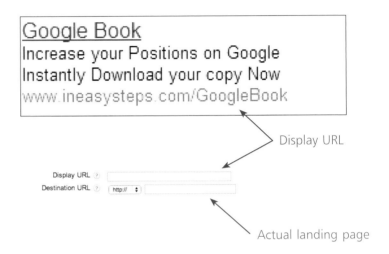

The display URL is not the URL of the page that the searcher will be taken to, but it will help to build in some more relevance and so will help us.

It is also important to note that you should not always take the searcher to your home page. In fact the home page is usually a page you would not want to take a searcher to.

You should try and take the searcher to the most relevant page on your website; this will further increase the relevance for them of clicking on your ad.

If the ad is for a "Google book" and you have a bookshop full of books, you would want to send that searcher directly to the page on your website that describes only the "Google book".

This helps to confirm to the searcher that they have made the right decision; you are helping them to find what they are looking for more quickly.

Keyword Research

Your keywords are the words or phrases for which you wish to have this particular ad shown.

It is important to remember that you will need to create separate ads for each service or product so you should only enter keywords that are specific to this ad.

When selecting keywords, remember to make use of those you have previously identified from your keyword research and analysis.

To choose your keywords you have several options:

- Enter specific phrases

- Find related keywords by using the search facility

- Scan Google's suggested categories based on a scan of your website

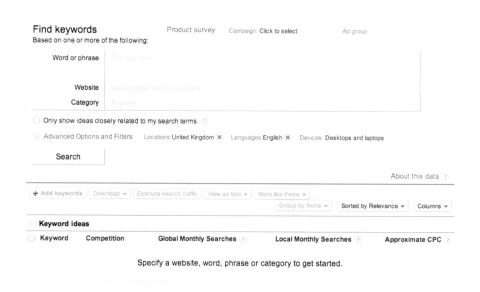

Once you have decided on your keywords, save them into a list so that you can enter them into the relevent ad groups that you will be creating.

Be sure to refer back to page 34 and also to refer to your organic keywords to ensure that you are targeting them all.

Match Types

Google AdWords not only allows you to choose the keywords for which you wish to appear, but also gives you tools to help you control how general or specific you need them to be.

These tools are called keyword matching options. There are four different types of keyword matching options. They will allow you to focus your keywords better.

Hot tip

Use exact match with incorrectly spelt keywords to canvass lost traffic.

▼ Advanced option: match types
Use these formats to make your keywords more precise [?]

```
keyword    = broad match
[keyword] = exact match
"keyword"= phrase match
-keyword  = negative match
```

Broad match

This is the default option when you implement your keywords. The broad match option means that whenever a search is made that contains all of your specific keywords, your ad will be shown.

"Phrase match"

This option means that your ad will only be shown if your keywords are searched for in the order you have written them. Your ad will still appear if other keywords are present in the query but only if yours are in order and together.

[Exact match]

This option means that your ad will only be shown when your exact search phrase is entered.

-Negative match

This option is used when there are specific keywords for which you do not want your ad to appear. Most businesses would use "–free" as a negative keyword to minimize the number of customers looking for free products.

The use of these keyword matching options can help you reduce your unwanted and unprofitable clicks, which will help to increase your return on investment (ROI).

Quality Score

AdWords introduced Quality Score to help decide which position an ad should be displayed in, to not rely on just how much the advertiser is bidding.

Each time a keyword is searched for, Google attribute a Quality Score between one and ten (with one being the lowest) based on a number of factors, including:

- Keyword relevancy
- Landing page quality
- Landing page load time

You can see your keyword within the main AdWords interface. The below screenshots show examples, with one and two keywords, one with a good Quality Score and the other with a bad one, detailing the problems with each keyword and what to do to fix them:

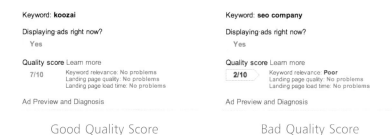

Good Quality Score   Bad Quality Score

Hot tip

The higher your Quality Score the lower your clicks will cost.

There are many optimization techniques that you can use to improve your quality score including:

- Add keywords to the headline of your ad
- Include the keywords in the body of your ad
- Add any promotions mentioned in an ad to the landing page
- Drive ads to the most relevant page not just the home page
- Ensure you have a privacy policy linked from the page
- Ensure the page loads as fast as possible
- Avoid using redirects, always send clicks to the actual page

Creating an Ad Group

1 First you need to name your ad group. Ensure that you use a relevent and memorable name as you will create many and need to be able to tell them apart

2 You now need to create your ad using the techniques outlined in the previous pages

You only need to create a text ad as the others are only used on the Display Network

Use your keywords in your headline

Ensure you use call to actions and state USP's in your description

Use your keywords in your display URL

Enter the URL you want the searcher to be taken to

This is what your ad will look like if it is displayed at the top of the results listings

This is what your ad will look like if it is displayed in the side results listings

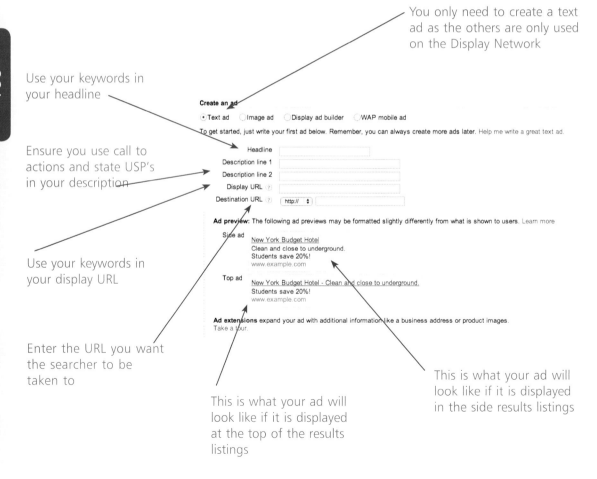

3 Now select your keywords for this ad group based on the process outlined on page 163 and not forgetting to use the match types - page 164

Keywords

☐ Select keywords
Your ad can be displayed on Google when people search for the keywords that you choose here.

When creating your keyword list, think like your customers: how would they describe your products or services? Specific keywords (often containing 2-3 words) will help you show your ads to the most interested users. Try starting with 10-20 keywords. You can always expand or refine later. Help me choose effective keywords.

Enter one keyword per line. Add keywords by spreadsheet

Help me choose effective keywords.

```
Add your keywords here
```

Estimate search traffic

Advanced: learn how to use keyword match types for more control.

Important note: We cannot guarantee that these keywords will improve your campaign performance. We reserve the right to disapprove any keywords that you add. You are responsible for the keywords that you select and for ensuring that your use of the keywords does not violate any applicable laws.

4 You now need to set your default bid for each click, remember you won't pay any more than your daily budget

Ad group bids

Maximum cost per click (Max. CPC)
You can influence your ad's position by setting its maximum cost-per-click (CPC) bid. This bid is the highest price you're willing to pay when someone clicks on your ad. You'll input an initial bid below, but you can change your bid as often as you like. Try a bid now to get started, then revise it later based on how your ads perform.

Default bid ⑦ $ 1.00
You can set keyword-level bids separately.

Display Network bid (optional) $ [   ] - Off
Leave blank to use your default bid (or keyword bids if you set them). ?

💡 **This ad group isn't quite ready yet. Before your ads can run, you'll need to complete the following tasks:**

- Create at least one ad.
- Add at least one keyword.

If you like, you can save this ad group without completing these steps and finish them later.

5 You have now set up your ad group and should review thoroughly before clicking "Save and continue to billing"

| Save and continue to billing | Set up billing later | Cancel new ad group |

Billing

All there is left to do to set your account live is to update your billing information.

To do this follow the below steps:

1 Select your country from the below drop down list

Account Setup

1. **Select the country or territory where your billing address is located.**
This choice may affect the payment options you will have in the next step.

Select a country or territory: ⇕

Continue »

2 Input your billing details and click "Continue"

Set up your billing profile

Business information

Business address ⑦
Business name
Optional
Contact name ⑦
Street address

Town/City
State ▾
Zip code
Country   United States
Phone number   +1

« Back   **Continue »**

3 Select automatic payments to ensure your ads don't get cut off and enter your payment information

4 Read through Google's terms and conditions and click Yes if you agree, and then Continue which will activate your account

12 Test and Measure

Running regular reports will ensure your AdWords account is running efficiently.

Landing Pages

Landing pages can be very useful in conjunction with Google AdWords.

You are at Google's mercy with the natural listings. With AdWords, however, you can select the specific page you want to direct your advert towards. To make the most of this you can create pages that are tailored to the searcher's specific query.

Effective landing pages

Hot tip

Remove navigation to restrict responses.

- Are relevant to the searcher's query

- Restrict navigation

- Speak to searchers, not at them

- Mention benefits

- Tell them what to do next

- Lead to purchase or enquiry

When you have created your new landing page you should use the Google ad split testing feature to test it to determine whether it is more effective than previous ads. This way you can modify the landing page again and again to improve its effectiveness.

Landing page aims

Hot tip

Landing pages need to be constructed to get a desired response so give visitors limited options such as Buy, Contact or Hit the back button.

- Get searchers' contact details via a form

- Convert searchers to customers

If you can get searchers to do this, you can measure your results and track them within AdWords. This will help you to work out how cost-effective your campaign is.

You really need to use your landing page to get the desired action, which will vary depending on what you are doing.

If you are selling products then you will be utilizing the landing page to encourage visitors to purchase the item. If you are selling services then you will want to get their contact details; with these you will be able to contact the lead and start the sales process.

Do not make the mistake of always trying to go for a sale.

Conversion Tracking

Conversion tracking is essential in order to see how truly cost-effective your Google AdWords campaign is.

Only when you have ascertained this can you really start seeing what's what when it comes to your account. Conversion tracking will even tell you exactly how much each conversion is costing you so that you can work out your overheads.

① Log in to your Google account

② Select AdWords from the Services menu

③ Now select "Conversions" from the "Tools and Analysis" tab

Tools and Analysis ▾	E
Change history
Conversions
Google Analytics
Website Optimiser
Keyword Tool
Traffic Estimator
Placement Tool
Contextual Targeting Tool
Ad Preview and Diagnosis

④ Click "New Conversion"

All conversion types
Last 7 days
9 Jan 2012 - 15 Jan 2012

| **Conversions** | Web pages | Settings | Code | Advanced |

+ New conversion | Imported from Google Analytics | Change status ▾

	Conversion ?	Conversion location ?	Category ?	Tracking Status ?	Conversions (many-per-click) ?	Value ?

Measure the value of your ad clicks
Your ads might be getting lots of clicks. But unless you know which clicks lead to valuable actions on your website, you're missing out on effective ways to optimise your campaigns.

With conversion tracking, you can track which keywords and clicks lead to certain actions - newsletter signups, downloads, purchases. This can show you the most effective keywords.

To set up conversion tracking:

1. Identify a web page that users reach after they've completed a valuable action on your website (such as the 'thank you' page that users see after they make a purchase).
2. Paste the HTML code that we generate for you into the web page (you can do it yourself or ask a webmaster).

Click the "New conversion" button above to get started!

Hot tip

Conversion tracking is a must for a financially efficient account; without it you have no idea what is generating leads or sales.

...cont'd

5 Give your conversion a name and select "Web page" before selecting "Save and Continue"

Conversion name	Settings	Generate code

Conversion name ⑦
Conversion location ⑦ ⦿Web page ○Call

Save and continue Cancel new conversion

6 Select the category you would like to put this conversion in from the list

Conversion category ⑦ ✓ Other
Page security level ⑦   Purchase/Sale
Conversion value ⑦   Signup
Optional   Lead
                          View of a key page

7 Select the page security level and if it is "HTTP" or "HTTPS"

Page security level ⑦ ✓ HTTP
Conversion value ⑦   HTTPS

8 Enter a conversion value if you would like to associate a value per conversion made

Conversion value ⑦
Optional

⑦ ⦿ Add a 'Google Site Stats' notification to the code generated for my page
This notification will appear only on the page that you add the conversion tracking code to.

Tracking indicator

Notification layout ○ Single line
                     ⦿ Two lines

Page background ⑦ #FFFFFF
colour

Notification Language ⑦ English ▾

Preview:
Google Site Stats
Learn more

○ Don't add a notification to the code generated for my page
Google recommends letting users know which pages you're tracking, either with a "Google Site Stats" notification or in your site's privacy policy.

9 Select to not add a notification to the code generated so no ad will appear on your website

10 Select "Save and continue"

Save and continue Cancel new conversion

11 Select if you will be implementing the code yourself or if you would like to email it to your developer

12 Copy and paste the code into your conversion page between the body tags

Beware

Your conversion tracking will not work if you do not implement the code correctly.

13 Your conversion tracking has now been set up. You can view this by navigating to AdWords, or wait for a customer to complete a conversion

Don't forget

This will have added two new columns to your report allowing you to see how much your conversions are really costing you.

Hot tip

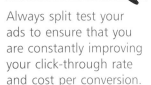

Always split test your ads to ensure that you are constantly improving your click-through rate and cost per conversion.

Split Testing

Split testing ads is an important part of increasing your conversions and reducing your cost per conversion.

Google allows you to set up your ad group with multiple ads so you can play them off against each other to see which one gives you the best results.

This is a continual process and you should always be playing ads off against each other.

To do this you must create two ads that are slightly different. Google will then serve both ads and feed back the results of both, which will enable you to tell which one is performing the best.

Once you have identified which is the inferior ad, you need to establish why and then improve it so that it outperforms the stronger one. This is something that you will need to work on, but it is a good way to ensure that your ads are generating the best possible response.

To start split testing your ads follow the steps below:

1 Navigate to the Campaigns page and select the campaign that you wish to split test

2 Select the ad group you want to split test from your campaign

3 Select which type of ad you would like to create in order to split test them from the "Ads" tab

4 You can now re-write your ad so that it will out-perform the existing one

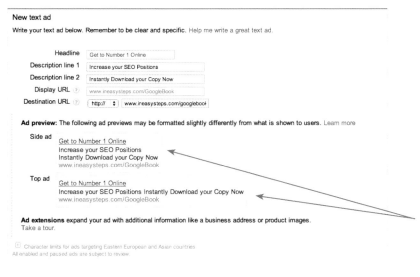

Ensure you check your ads to see how they will be displayed in the search results

5 When you are happy click "Save ad"

| Save ad | Cancel |

...cont'd

6 You now have another ad to split test against your existing ad

	Ad	Status ?	% Served	Clicks ?	Impr.	CTR ?	Avg. CPC ?	Cost	Avg. Pos.	Conv. (1-per-click) ?	Cost / conv. (1-per-click) ?	Conv. rate (1-per-click) ?	View-through Conv. ?
	Get to Number 1 Online Increase SEO Positions Now Instantly Download your Copy Online www.ineasysteps.com/GoogleBook ?	Under review	0.00%	0	0	0.00%	$0.00	$0.00	0	0	$0.00	0.00%	0
	Get to Number 1 Online Increase your SEO Positions Instantly Download your Copy Now www.ineasysteps.com/GoogleBook ?	Under review	0.00%	0	0	0.00%	$0.00	$0.00	0	0	$0.00	0.00%	0
	Total - search ?			0	0	0.00%	$0.00	$0.00	0	0	$0.00	0.00%	0
	Total - Display Network ?			0	0	0.00%	$0.00	$0.00	0	0	$0.00	0.00%	0
	Total - all ads			**0**	**0**	**0.00%**	**$0.00**	**$0.00**	**0**	**0**	**$0.00**	**0.00%**	**0**

Show rows [50 ‡] 1 - 2 of 2

7 Now you need to check your settings to ensure both ads will be evenly displayed by navigating to the "Settings" tab and selecting "Change campaign settings"

All online campaigns > New Campaign >
Ad group: **Google Book**

Get to Number 1 Online
Increase your SEO Positions
Instantly Download your Copy Now
www.ineasysteps.com/GoogleBook

View all 2 ads

○ Enabled
Ad group bids (Auto) ?
Default bid **$0.28**   Display Network bid **auto** ?

Settings Ads Keywords Networks Dimensions ▾

This ad group uses the settings from campaign 'New Campaign'. The campaign settings include budget, location and language targeting, and other settings that apply to all ad groups in the campaign.

Change campaign settings

Beware

If you don't set ads to rotate you won't get an accurate split test.

8 Now check that under the "Ad delivery" section it is set to "Rotate: Show ads more evenly"

⊟ Ad delivery: Ad rotation, frequency capping
  Ad rotation ? **Rotate: Show ads more evenly** Edit

Monitoring Your Results

Regular reports will help you to ensure that your figures are going in the right direction.

Google will allow you to create fully customized reports that will help you track things down to the minutest detail. You can save results and run the reports automatically – Google will even email them to you if you set them up correctly.

A very useful report to generate is a keyword report, as seen below:

Beware

If you do not run regular reports you will be wasting money.

1   Navigate to the Campaigns tab

2   Select the campaign you want to report on

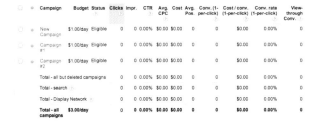

177

3   Select the "Keywords" tab

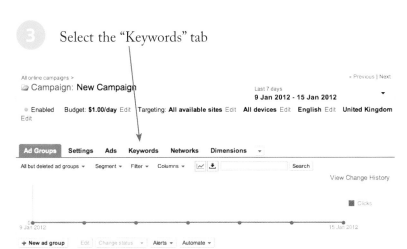

Hot tip

Regular reporting will help you maximize the efficiency of your account.

...cont'd

4 Now select the download button

5 Select a name for your report and decide whether you want regular email reports sent

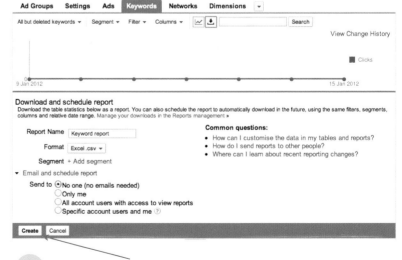

6 Now click "Create"

13 Google Places

Google Places is Google's business directory that utilizes Google Maps.

What is Google Places?

Google Places allows business owners with a physical address to update and manage their business listings.

The information provided will then be used to promote that business within Google Maps, associated Google properties and search and Display Network sites.

Google Places will show information pertaining to the business including:

- Business address

- Telephone number

- Website address

- Images and videos

- Opening times

- Map location

- Customer reviews

Every business with a physical location should be using Google Places as it has many benefits including:

- More coverage

- Greater opportunities to sell

- Another chance of your business ranking in Google

If you are a business with a physical location then you really need to have it listed on Google Places. This way you can be found in Google Maps and other associated Google properties.

Adding a Single Listing

If you would like to add your individual product to Google
Product Search follow the steps below:

1. Navigate to Google
   and search for
   "Google Places"

2. Select the Google
   Places Link

Google Places
www.google.com/places/
Google Places helps people connect with the places they love.

Google Places for Business	Places API
97% of consumers search for local businesses online. Be there ...	Supported Place Types - Places Autocomplete API - Places Library
Hotpot	QR Code
Places. Sign in to rate **places** and get personalized ...	What's that bar code? This unique bar code on the lower right of ...

More results from google.com »

3. Select the "Get Started"
   link from the "Get
   your business found on
   Google" section

📍 Get your business found on Google

Claim your business listing on Google - for free
Sign up for Google Places, or login to learn insights about your business.

[Get started ▸]

Hot tip

If you only have one
listing, this is how to
add it.

4. Sign in to your Google
   Account

Sign in
Email
[   ]
Password

[**Sign in**]   ✓ Stay signed in

Can't access your account?

5. Enter your country and phone number and then click
   find your business location

Google places | Settings | Help | Sign Out | English (United States)   :

Tip: Before you create a business listing, think about which Google Account you are using. In the future, you may want to share this account with other people at your business.

Enter your business's main phone number to see if Google Maps already has some information about your business. You'll then be able to edit any existing information and add new details, including photos and videos. About Google Places

Country	United States :
Phone Number	_____ [Find business information »]
	ex (201) 234-5678

Tip: Have more than 10 business listings?
Add them quickly by using bulk upload.

© 2012 Google · Google Home · Google Maps Home · Privacy Policy · Google Places Help · Google Places Home

To upload more than
ten listings select
"bulk upload" and
skip to page 185

6 If Google finds your address it will enter your address for you to confirm, if not, enter your address, phone number and main enquiries email address

Hot tip

Once you have entered your address ensure that the location is correct on the map.

▼ **Basic Information**

Please note that changing your address or business name will require additional verification via mail or phone.

* *Required Fields*

Country: *	United Kingdom
Company/Organization: *	
Street Address: *	
City/Town: *	
County:	
Postal Code: * [?]	
Main phone: *	
	Example: 0121 234 5678 Add more phone numbers
Email address:	
	Example: myname@example.com

---

7 Now enter your website details, a description of your business and up to five categories to list your business under

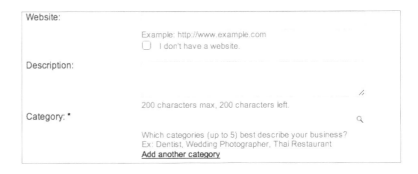

Website:	
	Example: http://www.example.com
	☐ I don't have a website.
Description:	
	200 characters max, 200 characters left.
Category: *	
	Which categories (up to 5) best describe your business?
	Ex: Dentist, Wedding Photographer, Thai Restaurant
	Add another category

8 Select "Service Areas and Location Settings"

▼ **Service Areas and Location Settings**

Does your business provide services, such as delivery or home repair, to locations in a certain area?

⦿ **No**, all customers come to the business location

◯ **Yes**, this business serves customers at their locations

9 Select your hours of operation

▼ **Hours of operations**

Make sure your customers know when you're open!

⦿ I prefer not to specify operating hours.
◯ My operating hours are:

Mon:	9:00 AM	-	5:00 PM	Closed ⇩ Apply to all
Tue:	9:00 AM	-	5:00 PM	Closed
Wed:	9:00 AM	-	5:00 PM	Closed
Thu:	9:00 AM	-	5:00 PM	Closed
Fri:	9:00 AM	-	5:00 PM	Closed
Sat:				✓ **Closed**
Sun:				✓ **Closed**

Are your hours split during a single day, such as 9-11am *and* 7-10pm?
I'd like to enter two sets of hours for a single day.

10 Select what types of payment you accept

▼ **Payment options**

Specify how customers can pay at your business.

☐ Cash ☐ Diner's Club ☐ Delta
☐ Check ☐ Discover ☐ Electron
☐ Connect ☐ MasterCard ☐ Eurocard
☐ Traveler's Check ☐ Visa ☐ Maestro
☐ Invoice ☐ Financing ☐ Solo
☐ American Express ☐ Switch ☐ Postal Order
☐ Paypal

...cont'd

11 Upload up to ten photos about your business and products

▾ **Photos**

Add flair to your listing: include photos of your products or your storefront. You can upload up to 10 photos. Please be sure they comply with our photo submission guidelines.

◉ Add a photo from your computer

[Choose File] No file chosen   [Add Photo]

◯ Add a photo from the web

You have uploaded **0** of up to **10** images for this listing.

12 Upload up to five business videos you have

▾ **Videos**

Enhance your listing by associating videos about your business. To do so, upload your video on YouTube and enter the URL below. You can include up to 5 videos.

[Add Video]

Example:http://youtube.com/watch?v=dFtfxv1JdXl

You have uploaded **0** of up to **5** videos for this listing.

13 Add any additional details such as parking etc

▾ **Additional Details**

Please enter in any other details you want customers to know about your business, for example:

Parking available: Yes.
Brands carried: Sony, Panasonic and Toshiba.

:   ☒

Add another

14 Preview your ad before submitting it   [**Submit**]

Don't forget

Your contact details will be shown on the internet.

184

Hot tip

Once you have submitted your ad you will get sent a confirmation letter by Google that you will need to activate to make it live.

Adding a Multiple Listing

1 Follow the steps on page 181 until you reach step five and click on "bulk upload"

2 Download the Google Places template file and review Google's formatting rules

3 Populate the template with your listings, save and upload, you will need to correct any errors before continuing

Upload Multiple Business Locations « Back to file upload

✓ **No Errors Found!** You can now publish your listings to Google Maps.

[Publish Locations]

Help us improve the upload process. Take our survey!

4 You can now click the "Publish Locations" button to submit your listings

Hot tip

If you have more than one listing, this is how to add them.

Beware

Always preview your ad to ensure it is accurate before publishing it.

Hot tip

Once you have submitted your ad you will get sent a confirmation letter by Google that you will need to activate to make it live.

Claiming an Existing Listing

If you find there is already a listing for your business on Google Places then you need to claim it. To do this follow the below steps:

1 Navigate to Google and search for "Google Maps"

2 Select the Google Maps Link

Google Maps
maps.google.com/
Find local businesses, view maps and get driving directions in **Google Maps**.
Street View - Maps API - Maps Help - Rich Snippets for Local Search

3 Search for your business and see if it is returned, if not follow the process on page 181

4 On the top right you need to select the "Business owner" link (if it says "Owner-verified listing" it means someone has already claimed it). You can still claim it, just make sure no one else in the business has first

Print - Link - Edit this place - Business owner?

5 Select "Edit my business information" and click "Continue"

6 Complete the relevant steps on pages 181 – 184 to claim the listing

14　Web 2.0

Once you have set up and optimized your website, it's time to take it to the masses.

In the next chapter you will be introduced to some of the leading Web 2.0 online marketing resources and how to use them to maximize your website's online profile.

What is Web 2.0?

The term Web 2.0 (sometimes referred to as "social media") is used to describe a perceived second generation of web development and design.

The first generation of the Web was largely focused on connecting people to information. The second generation, Web 2.0, was developed to facilitate communication between people.

Web 2.0 allows more than just the receiving of information; users can interact with these websites, commenting on information they find and building sites and resources to further increase the information available.

Some popular Web 2.0 sites include:

- Facebook

- YouTube

- Campfire

- Flickr

- Slide

- Blogger

- Digg

- Del.icio.us

- StumbleUpon

- Skype

- Wikipedia

- FeedBurner

- Ecademy

- LinkedIn

Web 2.0 has changed the way people use the Internet and opened up many avenues through which you can market your website online.

Beware

It is very important that you do not spam social sites; their users will turn on you, which will result in bad publicity for your website.

Hubs and Lenses

Hubs and lenses are a great way of promoting your website and building links at the same time.

Hubs and lenses are web pages that you create on a chosen topic which are then published through a community with your author's bio.

There are many benefits to creating hubs and widgets including:

- Traffic from another source

- More visitors to your website

- Promotion of yourself and your website

- Increased link popularity

There are many of these types of sites around but the two main sites I would recommend are:

- http://hubpages.com

- http://www.squidoo.com

HubPages is very easy to use and you can simply log in, create your account and then you are free to create your lens and promote it to the world.

Squidoo is very similar except their pages are referred to as lenses but they are in effect pages that you can create and publish within their community.

With Squidoo, once you have created your account you are free to create a lens, add links and any widgets you wish to and then you can publish it.

Squidoo will not feature your lens within its network straight away, but hold it as a work-in-progress lens. You will have to promote the lens through blogging and bookmarking etc. and encourage people to visit it to show that its content is strong.

Once you have shown that your content is strong, Squidoo will convert it to a featured lens and start promoting it within the community.

Hot tip

Be sure to spend time creating a good page otherwise it will generate minimal traffic and your work will have been in vain.

Social Bookmarking

Social bookmarking (sometimes referred to as "tagging") is a very popular Web 2.0 pastime, enabling you to have your bookmarks at hand wherever you may be.

Social bookmarks work in much the same way as normal bookmarks except that they are stored as a web page on the server rather than on your PC.

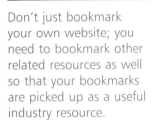
Before the advent of Web 2.0, you could only access a saved bookmark from the PC on which you had saved it. Social bookmarking was then born and people found they could bookmark all of their favorite websites and access them from any computer, anywhere in the world. And by tagging those bookmarks with relevant keywords, others could also find these resources much more easily and quickly through the network.

Digg is one of the leading social bookmarking sites and has a very simple way of scoring bookmarks. Once added its users can "digg" a bookmark they like, pushing it up Digg's internal rankings or they can "bury it" if they don't like it, sending it down the rankings.

Digg is therefore able to minimize the risk of its results becoming corrupted. The term "Digg effect" has been coined as a result of the enormous amount of traffic a website can receive after making the top spot on Digg's internal rankings.

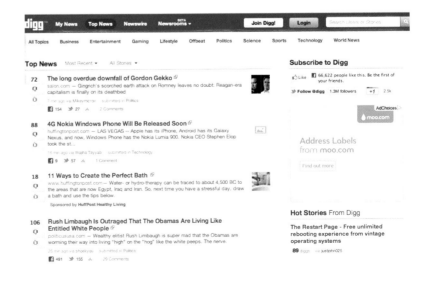

There are many social bookmarking websites out there and some target set niches; if you can find one it would be worthwhile using it.

Although all of the social bookmarking sites have different features, they all tend to follow the same set-up process:

1 Sign up for an account

2 Personalise your account by adding information about yourself and a picture

3 Download the services toolbar or browser plugin to make the process of tagging easier

4 Put your login details into the toolbar or plugin, to enable it to work

Hot tip

If you have a good website and can get lots of people to bookmark it, you will normally see your rankings improve.

Social bookmarking is also being used by the search engines to find new content and to decide how popular it is.

If many people are bookmarking a certain resource using relevant tags then the search engines deem it must be a credible resource and its rankings will probably increase.

Users' bookmarks are stored on their profile page. These bookmarks are classed as links so anyone can navigate and subscribe to them, in turn creating another link to that page.

Through using social bookmarking you can:

● Navigate your bookmarks from any PC with an internet connection

● Get your links picked up by the social networking services

● Increase the traffic to your bookmarked page

● Help others looking for related resources to find your bookmarked pages

Wikis

Wikis are Web 2.0 sites that have their pages and content both created and edited by their users.

Wikipedia is the foremost and best known wiki and holds incredible weight with Google.

Hot tip

A link from Wikipedia is worth its weight in gold so if you can legitimately get one, then spend the time to do so – it will be well worth it.

Wikipedia links are very valuable and there is, naturally, a great demand for them. Because of this, spammers continuously strive to get undeserved links.

Wikipedia combats this with its ever-growing army of volunteer editors who review changes to pages to ensure they are relevant and in the best interest of the cause.

A mention and link from Wikipedia will afford you many benefits including:

- One of the best quality inward links available

- Increased credibility within your niche

- A possible boost in PageRank

- Increased traffic from Wikipedia itself

If you have something of value on your site that an existing article could benefit from, it will be well worth the time invested.

However if you are trying to spam just to get a link, do not waste your time as it will be spotted and removed very quickly.

Twitter

Twitter is a service which allows you to keep people up to date with what you are doing.

It is a very easy to use service where you can follow people of your choosing and be followed by people who know you or people who just like what you have to say.

When you update Twitter as to what you are doing it will then send a "tweet" to everyone following you to let them know.

Although this may seem a purely social thing to do, which it is, it is also a very good way of getting traffic to your website.

Twitter has some great benefits including:

- The ability to get content reviewed quickly
- Increasing traffic to your website
- Gathering opinions, ideas and points of view
- Promoting your web links

By following and being followed by people interested in what you do, particularly those in a similar industry, you can greatly increase your profile.

This way when you release a new service, product or have some great news you can deliver it straight to your core audience and also send a link to make it easier for them to view.

Don't forget

You really want to get people following you that are interested or related to your niche to make this advertising vertical as effective as possible.

Video Sharing

Video has become very popular online with more and more people choosing to watch on their laptop or PC.

Google has now started to include more video results in line with its normal natural results so there is a chance that a well-optimized video could land you a top position on Google.

There are four stages in your video production/promotion and they are as follows:

Ideas stage

You need to decide what your video is going to be about and there are many ways to target your audience including:

- "How to" style

- Informative video about a certain topic

- Advertisement

- Case studies and testimonials

If you decide to create a video to promote your business, I would recommend a "How To" style. These videos are much more likely to go viral and the resulting buzz will see your rankings quickly improve.

Video creation

Once you have come up with an idea for your video, it's time to start creating. The best way I have found to present a "How To" clip is through the use of screen capture as you can record the screen you are looking at. This way, you can go through web pages and even PowerPoint presentations all in the same video.

I recommend Camtasia which you can get on a 30-day trial at http://www.techsmith.com/camtasia.asp.

When creating your video you need to ensure that you:

- Keep it under 4 minutes long

- Record it at the same size as it will be played back

- Use an external microphone to ensure good sound quality

Don't forget

Ensure that your videos are top quality or they may have a negative effect for your brand online.

Video editing and rendering

Once you have your raw footage you need to go though the process of cleaning it up before you create the final, finished video file.

When rendering the video you need to ensure that:

- The file type is compatible with where you are planning to upload it

- The file size is under 100 MB

- The title, description and filename contain the keywords your video is targeting

Video promotion

Now you have your final optimized video file it is time to share it with the world.

There are many video sharing websites out there including the giant that is YouTube.

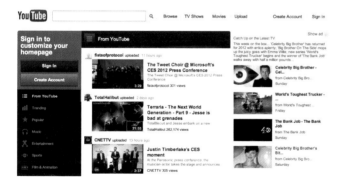

To submit to YouTube, like any video sharing site, you will need to sign up for an account and then follow the onscreen instructions to upload your video, ensuring you use your keywords in your titles and description as you would a normal web page.

If you are planning to create and promote multiple videos and would like to submit them to multiple video sharing websites, there are services available that will speed the process up for you such as www.trafficgeyser.com but these services do charge.

Hot tip

Don't just submit to YouTube as there are many niche video sharing websites out there that may be more focused on your area.

195

Photo Sharing

Photo sharing is something that may not be applicable for everyone but in certain circumstances it can be very useful.

Flickr is one of the leading photo sharing websites on the internet and it is incredibly easy to get your photos uploaded and online.

Don't forget

Use keyword-rich anchor text for the links that go to your website.

Using photo sharing websites gives you an increased chance of having your images picked up and returned in Google's image search results which can in turn deliver some really good quality traffic.

As an example, if you sold cameras, you could take pictures of the different cameras and their component parts and then include a keyword-loaded deep link to take the searcher through to your website.

Using photo sharing sites has some great benefits including:

- Relevant traffic from the site
- Keyword-rich backlinks to your website
- Expansion of your online profile
- Increased chance of rankings under a Google image search

Flickr is very easy to use but to get the most out of it you should ensure that you use:

- Descriptive titles for your photos
- High quality images
- Descriptive links to link to your pages

Social/Business Networking

One of the most effective ways to build a powerful online profile in your niche is to become an authority on your subject on the leading social and business networking websites.

LinkedIn is recognized as one of the leading business networking sites and is a great way of staying in touch and making new business connections.

Hot tip

Ensure you complete your profile fully as it will enhance your chances of being ranked higher on LinkedIn.

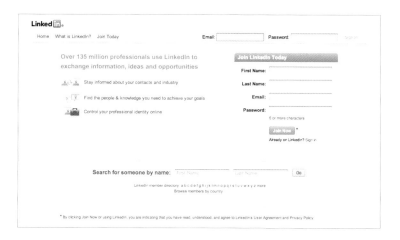

By using LinkedIn you can:

- Increase your online visibility in your particular niche

- Connect to new business contacts

- Gain backlinks from your profile page

- Connect with lost business contacts

- Display recommendations to people visiting your profile

I suggest spending some time setting up your profile page and keeping it professional and focused on your niche.

By doing this your profile will attract people interested in your core business and will therefore be more effective. You will also find that if set up correctly, LinkedIn can be a good source of business leads.

It is very important to also show some recommendations on your profile as these will boost your credibility and increase the chances of someone contacting you.

Facebook

Facebook is without a doubt one of the most powerful social networks in the world.

Although Facebook is used as a social application it also has some great ways to help your business.

The first way is to create a page for your business and include information about who you are and what you do. When you have this you can start getting people to "Like" your page. Once someone "Likes" your page you can then begin to communicate with them via the pages updates. This is a very good way of building up trust and brand reputation.

The second way is to advertise through Facebook's system and attract people through to your company's Facebook page. This, obviously, costs but the costs are quite low and can be a very efficient way of getting people aware of your business.

Using Facebook has some great benefits including:

- Create a real brand
- Interact with your customers and gain feedback
- Advertise direct to your customers through Facebook
- Another chance of ranking in a Google search

To get the most out of Facebook ensure you:

- Keep it professional
- Update regularly
- Include photos, videos, blog posts etc

Hot tip

You can link your blog to Facebook so it publishes your posts automatically.

Google+

Google+ is Google's social networking platform which has taken elements of Facebook and Twitter and incorporated them together.

There are certain key functions within Google+ including:

- Google Circles
- Google Hangout
- Google+ Pages

Google Circles enable you to group your relationships into circles, such as clients, friends, work colleagues etc making it easy to share content and updates to specific groups of users.

Google Hangout allows video conferencing with groups of up to ten people which is helpful for meetings with multiple users.

The most useful part for businesses has to be Google+ Pages. This feature allows businesses to create a page about their business that can then be integrated into the Google+ platform.

This is useful because people can then add the company's Google+ Page to their circle and start receiving regular updates.

Hot tip

Ensure you group your contacts into specific groups as this will help to ensure you send updates to the appropriate users.

199

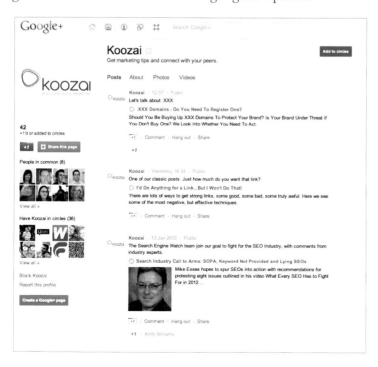

Blogging

Blogging has become a very popular medium for people to communicate both opinions and knowledge online.

Many companies also have blogs where clients and people with a general interest can stay up to date with what the company is doing, their ethos and any recent events.

Many blogs allow other people to contribute. The blog below resulted in the company discovering a unique way of using a free service rather than one they had previously paid for. This advice was shared, and further comments and ideas came in from different users who then left their names and links to their websites.

Main blog post →

Users comment →

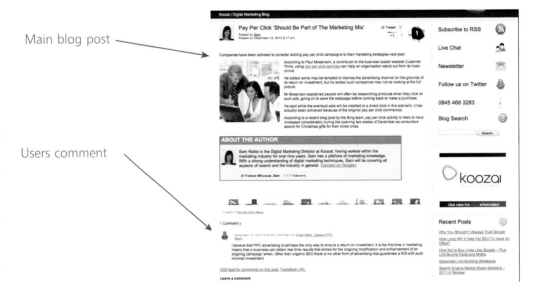

Commenting on others' blogs can be a very good way of:

- Increasing links to your website
- Increasing your profile online
- Sharing information
- Staying up to date on other people's opinions

As you can see, although it is a good idea, you do not always need to have your own blog. You can derive great benefits from contributing on others.

15 Extra Help

Find extra help with the optimization of your website.

Hiring a Specialist

Sometimes you will want to hire a specialist to ensure that your site is working at its optimum level.

Reasons to hire a specialist

- You need extra help because your industry is very competitive

- You do not have time

- It would be more expensive for you to do it yourself

The last option is the most common reason and yet the most often overlooked. There is a misconception that if you do things yourself you will save money.

This is not always the case as you need to assess how much your time is worth. You must then look at how long it will take you to optimize your website and work out whether you would earn more money doing other work in that amount of time.

It could be more cost-effective (and sometimes cheaper) for you to spend your time doing your normal job while paying a specialist to take care of the optimization of your website.

It is important therefore that you hire the right person for the job. By the right person we mean someone who knows what they are doing and who will only use ethical means.

Before you hire anyone to work on the optimization of your website make sure that they can give you the correct answers to the following questions:

- Do you only perform ethical optimization?

- Can I see some examples of your work?

- What rankings have you achieved for your clients?

- Do you optimize for keywords that bring real traffic?

- Will I get a report to explain what has been done?

- Will I need a monthly package to maintain my results?

- Will I be able to contact you as and when I need to?

- Do you have a client I could contact as a reference?

Don't forget

Good specialists will be busy and you may have to wait a month or so for them to start work on your website.

As in any industry there are some unscrupulous companies and so-called specialists who will try to con you with different tricks such as:

Top ten listings but no traffic

This is a common trick and one that is normally not noticed until it is too late. Site owners get so fixated with top ten listings that they can neglect to check whether people actually search for their keywords.

To combat this ask the specialist whether you will receive a report outlining the keywords to be used and the expected monthly searches.

Hiding text on the page

Sometimes companies will hide text on your page to try and increase the relevance of that page. This does not work as Google can tell if the color of the text is the same as the background. If Google detects this you will be penalized and possibly removed from the search listings.

To ensure this has not happened to you, navigate to your page and choose Select All from the Edit menu on your browser.

Optimizing their own website with your money

Creating new and optimized sites is a tactic used to increase the dependency of your website. This is achieved by improving the PageRank of the new website and linking into your website from it. This in itself is acceptable but you must check that you own the website that they are working on. If you don't, you will be paying the company to optimize a site they own. If you stop using them they can turn off the links and take the site back.

They could even rent the site to a competitor, which would mean that you would have paid to develop a competitor's PageRank.

You will find that any reputable company or specialist will not mind these questions and you will not offend them by asking. If people react badly to these questions then it is not a good sign and I would suggest you carry on searching for an alternative company.

Beware

If you're not convinced about a company or specialist then keep looking.

Getting Free Advice and Help

There are many ways to get further help and advice on your particular area of need but the most effective of these methods is through forums.

An internet forum is an online resource where people come together to hold conversations and ask as well as answer questions.

It can sometimes seem a difficult task to get answers to your specific questions but with forums it's easy.

Forums operate like an online community where people can come together and meet to discuss topics of mutual interest.

Forum benefits

- It is normally free to join a forum and remain a member
- The forum will be on your desired subject
- It is a fast way to get free answers to your specific questions
- There is usually a friendly and easy-to-use interface
- The people on the forum will range from those with no knowledge to specialists in the field
- You can create incoming links to your site through your own customized signature

There are many forums on search engine optimization but the most effective ones I have found are:

- http://www.webworkshop.net/seoforum/index.php
- http://forums.seochat.com/
- http://forums.searchenginewatch.com/

To get going on a forum you will simply need to navigate to it and select the "create a new account" option.

From there you will be asked to enter your relevant details and create your account. Once you have done this you can start chatting and asking questions.

Hot tip

Forums will help you increase your knowledge and inward links at the same time.

Beware

Do not attempt to spam or over-sell yourself on your forum or you will become very unpopular and could risk being banned.

Google's Sandbox

The Google sandbox is a concept that has been coined to describe the effect that new websites have in Google's search results.

New websites do not behave in the same way as older, more established websites in Google's search results.

It seems that Google is less inclined to rank newer websites until they have proved themselves and gone through a "probationary" period. This seems to be a period of between 90 and 120 days.

This is not to say that everything you do is pointless within this time, it just means that your efforts will probably be put on hold until this period has passed.

The Google sandbox could be used by Google for many things other than just new websites. Google could also use this for websites that it believes are not playing fair or that have suddenly gained large numbers of inward links.

If you have a new website, you should make your changes and optimize it gradually. This includes building links to your website.

You should try to build links slowly over time instead of adding a hundred in one sitting. This sudden spike of inward links could cause you problems. It would look unnatural, as links are not normally achieved this fast.

There are several ways you can deal with the Google sandbox and its effects, including:

- Use an existing, older domain name instead of buying a new one

- Build links slowly over time

- Optimize your website slowly

- In the early days, concentrate on other search engines

- Utilize pay per click (PPC) for your initial placements

The Google sandbox effect is not a recognized algorithm by Google; it is just a phrase to describe the effect often seen with new websites that have only recently been found by Google.

Hot tip

Be patient with new websites as they will need time to mature before Google will rank them at their full potential.

205

Beware

Do not build links too quickly with a new website as it will look unnatural to Google.

Google's Trustrank

Google's trustrank is an algorithm believed to determine search engine positions. It apparently assesses your website to see how trustworthy it is in order to improve the effectiveness and relevance of its search results.

There are many things that could affect your trustrank including:

- Domain age

- Number of links you have

- PageRank of the websites that link to you

- Trustrank of the sites that link to you

- Controversial topics such as gambling or pornography

- Spam on your site or sites that link to you

- Length of a domain registration

- Regular updating

- Unique IP address

- Displaying a privacy policy

- Displaying contact details including an address

- Sitemaps

- Security certificates

Hot tip

Try to get links from well-respected websites like CNN and the BBC as this will help Google to see your website as trustworthy.

The main factors that will probably influence your trustrank are the age of your domain and the quality of the websites that are linking to you.

The main point to remember with both trustrank and PageRank is to ensure everything you do is for the right reasons and that it is ethical.

If you make sure you are not doing anything that you believe could be interpreted as bad practice, the chances are your website will be fine.

Google's trustrank is not recognized by Google as an existing algorithm; it is just a phrase to describe an effect often seen in practice.

Absolute Link
A complete URL that contains the domain name and extension of a website – normally used when linking to other sites.

Accessibility
The extent to which a website can easily be accessed by disabled people and also by search engines.

AdWords
A form of sponsored advertising on Google using pay-per-click ads to generate targeted traffic to your website.

Algorithm (Google's)
Google's secret set of criteria that it uses to analyze your website and define its search engine ranking position.

Alt tags
Strings of text that are used to describe website images to the search engines and screen readers.

Anchor text
Text on a web page that contains a hyperlink redirecting you to another page.

Article
A document used to relay information to its readers, and normally distributed and displayed on other related websites in exchange for a link to your site.

Backward link
Link from other relevant websites to your website, for which no return link has to be provided.

Black hat SEO
Unethical methods of search engine optimization.

Blog
An online journal used to post thoughts, commentary and news on a particular subject.

Browser
The program used to access and view websites. Examples include Internet Explorer, Firefox, Safari and Opera.

Cached page
Google's stored copy of a web page.

Campaign
A group of AdWords ad groups in your Google AdWords PPC account.

Cascading style sheet (CSS)
An external style sheet used to store the structure and formatting of your web pages.

Cloaking
A black-hat SEO technique where website content displayed to a search engine spider is different from the content presented to the users.

Content
The information and data provided on your website in its main body area.

Conversion rate
The percentage of visitors viewing your website who then complete a desired action, e.g. a sale.

CPC
The maximum cost per click you will pay when your ad is clicked on.

CTR
The percentage of time your ad is clicked on compared to how often it is shown.

Directory
A website displaying a list of other websites that are grouped into specific categories.

Domain name
The name of your website, for example www.ineasysteps.com.

Doorway page
A page created for spamming search engine indexes with the purpose of redirecting you to another page when a particular search phrase is used.

Dreamweaver
A program used to design and edit web pages.

Dynamic website
A site where the content is created dynamically from a database instead of being stored in static web pages.

External links
Links to other websites from your own website.

Flash
Technology that uses a free plug-in to allow your browser to display animations and Flash movies as you navigate the web.

Form
Used to collect information from your visitors then sent to a specified pre-determined location.

Forum
A facility on the internet used to hold discussions and post information regarding a specific topic.

Frames
Outdated technology used to create websites.

Google Places
A business directory that displays companies related to a specific search query based on location.

Guestbook
A logging system that allows people visiting your website to leave a public comment.

Header tags
Used to format the text sizing on web pages to help add structure and outline the main section headings.

Home page
The main page on your website, also known as the index or default page.

Hosting provider
A company that provides space on its server to enable you to make your website accessible to all on the World Wide Web.

HTML Hyperlink
Part of a web page that when clicked on will display a different page, the address of which is specified in the link.

Internal links
Links that are placed on a website and used to navigate around it.

Keywords
The words and search phrases targeted when optimizing your website.

Landing page
The specific page your visitors are directed to after clicking on an ad.

Latent semantic indexing
Technology used to determine words that are related, to help build relevance.

Linkdex
Software used to help analyze and optimize your website and check your rankings.

Link farm
A large number of websites that all link to each other for the purpose of spamming the search engines.

Meta description
The description you have provided in your website to be shown in the search engines.

Meta tags
The tags you have used to describe your website to the search engines.

Meta title
The tag shown in the search engine ad to describe your website and which is also shown at the top of the page.

Natural listings
Search results in Google where the free "organic" search results are displayed.

Off-the-page optimization
The optimization of backward links and of what other websites are saying about your site.

Online competition
The top listed websites for your chosen keywords.

On-the-page optimization
The optimization of your website's content and structure.

Organic search
See Natural listings.

PageRank
A score that Google gives your web page depending on the quantity and quality of your inward links.

PPC (sponsored listing)
Pay per click: the area in Google used to display paid listings.

Reciprocal link
A link offered to another website on the understanding that your site will receive one in return.

Redirect
When one web page is set up to direct its visitors straight to another page.

Relative link
A link that takes visitors to a different page within the same website. Relative links do not contain complete URLs.

Resource page
A page where you will place related links to other relevant websites.

Root folder
The main folder on your web server. This will be where your home page is located.

Sandbox
The effects seen with new websites in Google's search results.

Screen readers
A program that presents web content to visitors who cannot see it.

SEO
Search engine optimization, the process of optimizing your website to appear in a better position within the natural search engine listings.

Search engine spider
The robot that Google sends out to crawl the web by going from website to website via links.

Server
The place where your website is stored online and to which you will upload your changes.

Sitemap
A page on your website that includes a list of all your pages, to enable good navigation.

Site submission
The submission of your website to the search engines.

Source code
The code used to create your website, which is also analyzed by the search engines.

Spamming
Any technique used to falsely improve a website's position in the search engine listings.

Split testing
The testing of ads or landing pages against each other to increase efficiency.

Static website
A website that is updated manually via the use of software or HTML.

Traffic
The numbers of visitors and search engine spiders reaching your website over a given amount of time.

Typo spam
The use of misspelt keywords and/or domain names to canvass lost traffic.

URL
Uniform resource locator. The address of a page on a website that identifies it on the World Wide Web.

Validation
The process of ensuring that a website conforms to the rules and guidelines laid out to ensure its accessibility to disabled visitors.

W3C
The World Wide Web Consortium where the rules and guidelines for accessibility are agreed.

Website structure
The layout and structure of your website's pages, files and folders.

Website theme
The main focus of your website's content.

Index

M

N

O

P

Q

R